ALEXANDRA JOHN

BEING YOUR OWN BOSS

How to start up a business

Disclaimer:
The information included in this book is only of an informative nature.
The author and the publisher are not to be held liable for its accuracy,
especially regarding information from external sources. The author
and the publisher are not to be held liable for your actions.

ALEXANDRA JOHN   Being your own boss
Text © Alexandra John
ISBN: 978-80-906584-0-0

Contents

Introduction

DEAR READERS AND FUTURE BUSINESSWOMEN,
You are on the first page of a book that will guide you through your entrepreneurial beginnings. You might not be sure that you've made the right decision, or you may already be feeling the fresh winds of change. Yes, starting up a business will bring great changes to your life. Just think about how many people waste their opportunities, sweep them under the carpet refusing to move off the beaten track. You are the one who is searching for new ways, trying to do things differently, and I appreciate it!

I'm trying to imagine who you are: you may have just graduated from university, you may have many years of employment behind you, or you may be just about to end your maternity leave. Whatever the case may be, you feel the urge to show the world what is hiding inside you, to take responsibility for your life and stand on your own feet. And earn money, naturally!

I dare say I know what you're going through. I was driven to write this book by my own personal experience. When I graduated I knew only one thing for sure: I wanted to be an entrepreneur. But I had no idea where or how to start. I didn't know what it takes to be an entrepreneur and there was no one around me I could ask for advice. I was searching for my own way, and one day I launched a job website. The fact that I was later forced to end this project was a valuable experience for me. Even if you don't succeed at the first attempt, don't beat yourself up about it. Instead, think about what you should do differently next time (change your business model, procedures, scope of business or something else) and give it another try. Don't give up too easily!

After many years of hard work, my husband and I built Meriglobe Advisory House Ltd., a successful London-based international company providing consultancy services to businesspeople. Over those years I met many company owners who were dealing with various problems, facing their failures and losses, but also enjoying their successes and victories. Meeting them was a valuable experience. There's a solution to every situation, even though we may not see it at the time.

There's one more thing. There are some women among our clients, but female entrepreneurs are still as scarce as hens' teeth. Although the number of women in company management has been increasing in the past decades, many people still think the epitome of a top manager is a man. This mentality is widespread, despite the fact that sex is not an important aspect of being a manager, or even a company boss. What is important is the ability to lead people and the knowledge acquired from experience in management. It doesn't matter if the boss is a man or a woman. Tradition has it that men are usually good leaders and visionaries and that they are more competitive and combative, which is sometimes counteracted by their oversized egos and rather limited empathy and adaptation. It is also said that women are more intuitive, less argumentative, good listeners, more empathetic and more patient. They can thus manage their company and their team just as well as men, although in a different way.

Madeleine Albright once said that there is a special place in hell for women who don't help other women. I strongly agree with her, which is why you are now holding in your hands this book containing the essential information and specific steps you need to take when starting up your business. I wrote it to support you, all the women who are thinking of setting up their own businesses. Don't be afraid to do it, don't hesitate to believe in your capabilities and don't let anyone discourage you from accomplishing your goals. Should you want more tips and tricks or other real cases and stories, you can visit my website www.alexandrajohn.com, where women entrepreneurs, especially those at the start of their journey, will find a lot of useful information as well as opportunities to share their experiences and inspire each other.

In conclusion, I would like to emphasize that I don't encourage you to do business simply because I want you to "wipe the floor with men" in the name of the fight against social stereotypes! Do it only if you feel it is your personal calling. Entrepreneurship is a beautiful journey full of adventure and you don't know where it may take you. That is what makes it so exciting!

May this book be your best guide on your journey through entrepreneurship!

ALEXANDRA JOHN
Prague, London (December 2017)

Chapter 1

A businesswoman!
Are you talking about me?

Please come in and have a look around
to see what awaits you

When you hear the phrase "world economy", the first thing that will probably come to your mind is the word "crisis". You may be afraid to plunge into business in such uncertain times. But, frankly speaking, when is any time "certain"? The golden years are always those in the past. We're living in the here and now, and the present always has both its advantages and its drawbacks. It depends on what side of the coin you are looking at.

Moreover, economic crises are very similar to crises we face in our personal lives. Nobody is happy when they strike, but retrospectively we appreciate how much these hard times made us stronger and tougher. People will always have needs; all you need to do is to find a gap in the market and estimate whether you are able to fill it. An ailing economy sharpens your brain, your senses and boosts creativity and readiness for action!

Starting up a business in uncertain times when all entrepreneurs must reckon with great risks and learn to react quickly to changes is, of course, a challenge.

Even those who don't own a multinational company need to take into account – at least to a certain extent – climate change, progressive depletion of traditional energy sources and the political situation in many countries.

CONSCIOUS CONSUMERS WELCOME!

You certainly must have noticed that globalization is, slowly but surely, going out of fashion and the trend is to protect national economies. Many consumers have adopted the motto: "from global to local". There are still more and more people who, when they go shopping for certain kinds of goods, prefer taking a basket instead of a shopping trolley and heading to the farmers' market rather than the supermarket. We are rediscovering "our" regional bakers, butchers and greengrocers. We go to cafés where they cook using exclusively local products, we buy coffee from small private roasters and there are many other examples of products that we prefer to come from local sources rather than the other side of the world.

It is no longer just when it comes to food that we are thoughtful and conscious consumers who not only care about "what" we are buying but also "where from" and "how". We are more conscious of the origin, circumstances under which it was made and, above all, the quality of the product (it was not so long ago that the term "fair trade" was only familiar to a couple of enthusiastic idealists). Companies have come to understand that profit is not the only thing that matters, but that they should also live up to their obligations to society to score points with their customers.

You may argue that the most prosperous shops are those selling cheap goods from Asia, because most people are looking for the best prices. I don't deny this, but what I am talking about is the direction in which the development is heading. Of course, traits attributed to men, such as courage, speed, directness and willingness to take risks, are still important for success in business, but they alone are not enough. It is no coincidence that a new space is opening up for female entrepreneurs who imbue business with other values.

SMALL AND MEDIUM-SIZED COMPANIES ARE "IN"

What speaks in favour of enterprising women is also the fact that small and medium-sized companies are becoming the backbone of economies in Europe and elsewhere, as they are more flexible than large concerns and can adapt more easily to the quickly changing requirements of the market. Naturally, it always depends on what specific conditions there are for doing business in a particular country.

In many countries, entrepreneurs have to struggle with rather complicated and hard-to-digest legislation and a large administrative burden. Other complications include rather frequent and radical changes to tax laws and local corruption. For example, according to the Ministry of Industry and Trade of the Czech Republic, last year there were more than 10,000 new female entrepreneurs in the Czech Republic where women now account for more than a third of all entrepreneurs [1]. This trend is in line with developments in other countries as women whose destiny is to combine a professional career with a family are greatly helped by the fast development of information technology.

US investor and businesswoman Ingrid Vanderveldt believes that: "The economy will recover thanks to a new view, the view of women." Will you join in?

A FEMALE ENTREPRENEUR?
ARE YOU TALKING ABOUT ME?
CONSCIOUS CONSUMERS WELCOME!

It's nice to be your own boss – to work when and from where you want. Isn't that right?

Who wouldn't want to decide when to go to work, when to leave, what needs to be done during working hours and what can wait – or even have the option to decide not to work that day just because the weather is nice, it is your daughter's birthday or there is a rerun of the latest episode of your favourite TV series that you missed last night.

It doesn't matter that such plans will remain in the realm of fantasy and you will get down to work anyway. What matters is that you know you CAN and if you don't feel like working, you DON'T HAVE TO!

Naturally, there are several other advantages.

NO MORE NEEDLESS COMMUTING TO WORK!

Whether you start doing your business "online" or open a brick-and-mortar shop, fitness studio or language school, you will decide where it will be located. Often, this will save you a lot of time that you would otherwise have to spend commuting to and from work. You won't need to bother any longer with catching the bus or spending money on petrol. You're a busy woman and you certainly have more important things to do than travel there and back every day!

NO MORE DRESS CODES!

Nobody will be telling you what clothes to wear. Work in your track suit, night gown or your daughter's fancy dress. Whatever you feel most comfortable in when working. Paradoxically, some people say that in order to be able to work efficiently at home, they need to be wearing the same type of clothes they wore when they were employed. So grab a tailored suit or a track suit, it's up to you!

NO MORE FIXED WORKING HOURS!

Are you a night owl who feels like a zombie in the morning, or are you an early bird whose work performance drops in the evening? Do you need to pick up your kids from school or check on your ill aunt every morning? You don't need to worry any more about how to explain it to your boss or how to take an extra half-day off because there is a plumber coming to your house in the morning. When you are your own boss, you can determine the working hours that suit you best.

NO MORE BLIND OBEDIENCE TO YOUR SUPERIORS!

You don't need to do tasks that you consider useless or respect a process you disagree with just because your boss (who you possibly have no respect for) tells you to. You don't even have to watch, frustrated, how the management repeatedly ignores your recommendations. Decisions about the direction your company will be heading in, and how, are in your hands only. Now you only answer to yourself and nobody else.

NO MORE WORRIES OF GETTING THE SACK!

There is no need to worry whether or not you will lose your job just because you fall out of favour with your boss (or, alternatively, that you'll get unwanted advances) or because your colleague blames you for his mistake and the management doesn't believe you. Now you are the one who negotiates new orders, and you can choose who you will or won't deal and cooperate with.

NO MORE HANDING YOUR PROFIT OVER TO SOMEONE ELSE!

If you make the right decision, the profit goes to you. The fruits of your labour will go directly to your pocket, not to your boss, CEO, members of the board of directors or shareholders. Doing business also enables you to influence the level of your income.

When she was pregnant with her second child, Stephanie initially started her business as a way to replace the income she was losing while on maternity leave. "Not until I went back to work did I realize that I really wanted to make my business work", explains Stephanie, "so I started searching for what I could offer (in my expertise) that was also helpful and profitable." Having found the term "Virtual Assistant", she researched as much as she could on the industry and began to offer VA services. Stephanie's business has now grown into a successful consulting firm. (2)

(Stephanie Coradin, USA)

ARE YOU READY TO BE RICH?

When asked why they want to start a business, many women speak about self-actualization, making their dreams come true, a desire to arrange their life to their liking. Hardly any of them say: "I want to be rich." But having enough money for one's own needs and those of one's family is a legitimate reason to start your own business!

The truth is that as employees we have no chance to become rich. We all sell our time, and most of us do it by the hour. No matter if we earn ten pounds or ten thousand, our earnings are limited as we can only dedicate a limited number of hours per day to work. Then there is a second type of person who is not limited by time, but by a fixed amount of work for an agreed fee. They receive money for their ideas and actions. These are entrepreneurs who determine the price of their work themselves.

The question in the heading is not rhetorical. I really mean it: are you ready to get rich? I can hear you answering "yes", but this is not guaranteed. Try to imagine you are extremely wealthy. How much do you earn per month? How much money do you have and what do you intend to do with it? The immediate answers may surprise you. It might be hard to say aloud that you earn £50,000 per month. To your surprise you might find that you wouldn't know what to do with the money.

How would you describe your attitude to money? How often do you think about it? Do you know what your family budget is? Do you have an idea what your monthly expenses are? Do you like to stock banknotes in an envelope in a kitchen drawer? Or – no matter how hard you try – does your salary slip through your fingers each month? Without being aware of it, you act under the influence of behaviour patterns usually learnt in childhood. What did you hear from people around you when you were a child? Maybe it was one of these statements: "Money is dirty." "Business is just for the rich." "Money isn't important." "Stick to what you have." What is "your" behaviour pattern? Think about it.

Business is always about money, whether you like it or not. Establishing a company and not considering money important, whatever the reasons, is a recipe for failure, just like it is when somebody sets up a company only because of money. It is unlikely that anyone will be engaged over the long term for many hours a day, with maximum determination, in something they actually aren't interested in.

BEING YOUR OWN BOSS IS A GREAT RESPONSIBILITY

As I have already said, coins have two sides and business is no exception. In the following chapter we are going to talk about self-assessment, and we will discuss how you can find out if doing business is the right choice for you. Yes, it is important to realize that business is not for everyone! Even though you might like the advantages of being your own boss, you should also be aware of a number of other facts which we will look at now.

YOU ARE GOING TO HAVE TO MAKE UNPLEASANT DECISIONS

You will be the one running your own company and every single decision you take will influence your success. It is a great responsibility, and you will carry it on your shoulders alone.

You are going to have to make pleasant as well as unpleasant decisions and deal with various problems, often taking unpopular measures. There will be no boss above you who can relieve you of these obligations.

On the other hand, if you know what is good for your company, you can start straight away. You don't have to wait until your superior finally decides to take the plunge or watch helplessly as somebody else takes the wrong steps.

YOU WON'T GET PAID FOR "OVERTIME"

You will have to work many hours of "overtime", usually unpaid, at least at the start: a necessary sacrifice you have to make in order to achieve future success. And when you become tired, you can forget about having a rest as there will be nobody you can delegate the tasks to.

There will be nobody to entrust with solving the problems that will, sooner or later, arise. When you come across trouble, you will have to face it with determination, although you'd rather run far away from it.

WITH YOUR FAMILY BY YOUR SIDE, BUSINESS IS EASIER, BUT ALSO MORE COMPLICATED

If you have a family, doing business will be more difficult because you will have to have consideration for your partner and your children. On the other hand, your family will provide you with a sanctuary where you can recharge your batteries, relax and forget about work problems.

If you want to do business, you don't need special education, training or a certificate. All you need is genuine desire, effort, determination and common sense. As Moira Forbes, president of the ForbesWoman magazine and website said:

"Entrepreneurs don't just come up with ideas. They make things happen." This brings us to the most important question, which is why now is the best time to start up a business. Do you have an idea? Because if you do, it will only become valuable once you have turned it into reality.

"I'd never thought of being a freelancer. They've always laughed at me at home for being slow and being lost in my thoughts. I was used to obeying my parents, so after I graduated from college I dutifully picked a 'reasonable occupation' and started working in an office in administration. But, I couldn't wait to get home and do, finally, what I lived for. My passion was and still is writing. I set up a blog and started writing about what I was interested in – good food, fashion, travelling. After a couple of years, it grew into a successful business. The income from advertising amounts to thousands of pounds each month."

(Laura, 29, UK)

WHY YOU SHOULD LAUNCH YOUR BUSINESS RIGHT NOW

When is the right time to have a baby, buy a house or start up a business? In a week, three months, two years or a decade? As for a business, if you sit and wait and write lists of arguments for and against establishing your own company, you will always find enough things to discourage you. You mustn't mistake the right moment for the ideal moment, as that never comes. The right moment is when you feel that you are ready, irrelevant of external circumstances.

You see an opportunity that is worth pursuing.

I don't intend to prompt you to take a rash, impulsive decision. Naturally, you should "look before you leap". You need to consider all the possibilities and think everything over. But don't hesitate for too long – opportunities will not hang around forever. Consider whether you are really waiting because you are pondering your possibilities, or perhaps because you are afraid to take the first step.

For those who need to hear further convincing arguments in favour of starting a business, here are a few more in conclusion:

BEING A SMALL SHARK IS AN ADVANTAGE

As I mentioned at the beginning, economic situations change very quickly. Smaller companies can operate with lower overheads and are thus more qualified to overcome hard times.

WHERE THERE'S A COLLAPSE, THERE'S A BOOM

When the economy is on the decline or new technologies are being introduced, opportunities open up in many industries. While some industries are withering away, others are flourishing. "For instance, when Chrysler went bankrupt as its cars with high consumption stopped selling, Jitterbug, a company from San Diego making simple mobile phones for elderly people, hired new employees and grew at a sky-rocketing speed" [3]. In other words – your idea may get a better foothold now than at any other time

STARTING WITHOUT BURDEN

You are not limited by any prejudices or scepticism resulting from previous negative experience, whether yours or somebody else's. You are unbiased, unburdened with awareness of old business models, while sufficiently flexible so that you can adapt your business to customers' current requirements.

THE PERSONAL APPROACH IS "IN"

The current market favours small entrepreneurs. Potential customers want to negotiate with a real person, not a corporation. They prefer the personal approach, even when shopping online. Individuals don't want to feel like an anonymous entity in a uniform mass of customers or like just a number. And there is nothing easier for you to do than approach your clients individually.

QUESTIONS TO CONSIDER

 **WHAT WOULD BE THE MAIN ADVANTAGE IF I WERE MY OWN BOSS?**

This is an important question, because you need to be strongly motivated so that you are completely devoted to your business.

 **AM I READY TO RUN MY OWN BUSINESS?**

We've mentioned why it is important to start up a business right now, so now it is just appropriate to ask if you feel ready for it.

WHAT IS MY RELATIONSHIP WITH MONEY?

Succeeding in business is preconditioned by having a healthy and well-balanced relationship with money, so pay careful attention to this topic.

AM I READY TO FACE STRESSES, UPS AND DOWNS?
AM I READY TO INVEST AS MUCH TIME AS NEEDED?

Starting up a business is a big decision, so you'd better make sure you are ready for the long run.

Be honest when answering these questions. Take an unbiased look at whether you are ready to start up your own business. If you are, you need to be sure that business is the right thing for you. Do you have what it takes? We will go over that more thoroughly in the following chapter.

Chapter 2

Do you have a head for business?

Find out if business is in your blood

Considering running your own business is in many respects similar to preparing for parenthood. Not only do you need to get ready mentally and financially, but you also need to devote yourself to satisfying your child's needs until he or she becomes self-sufficient. And even then, your child will be dependent on you to a certain degree, regardless of age.

Starting your own business is a life-changing decision. In order to succeed, you will need motivation, determination, passion and time. If you have all of this, you can gain a lot in return – I'm not talking about money now, but about new experiences, skills, self-fulfilment and a sense of satisfaction or even contentment. But before you get down to business, you should first find out if you are ready for such great responsibility. If you have worked as an ordinary employee until now, it could be difficult for you to imagine what lies in store. Even if you have managerial experience, it doesn't automatically follow that you have a talent for business. I don't mean to discourage you; I just want to point out that running a business isn't simply about doing something different from what you've been doing so far. Most importantly, you will need to THINK DIFFERENTLY. Many university graduates make what we might call obedient employees. The challenge is to find personalities who think independently and creatively. Fortunately, this "new thinking" goes hand in hand with the rule that we learn from our mistakes and that if there's something we don't know, we can learn it.

"My grandparents used to run a restaurant. I remember running around wooden tables with checked tablecloths watching ladies nibbling at their dessert after lunch and gentlemen enjoying their beer from a dewy glass. The river murmured, the sun was shining, it was flawless. Later on, I studied architecture and settled down to a life at the drawing board. But I wanted to be with people and dreamed of having my own café. I made my dream come true after several years and the place worked just fine. However, I had to admit that although I did like fulfilling my guests' wishes, despite all my efforts I couldn't cope with the paperwork. It was ruining me more than I would have expected ... Well, there was a good outcome. My husband saw how worried I was and he offered to look after the paperwork so that I could focus fully on serving guests. I'm grateful to my husband as I see how he helped me and the restaurant."

(Marlene, 38, Germany)

I'm going to start with a list of questions that will help you create a picture of what it takes to be a company owner. (By a "company" I mean any business of whatever size ranging from a small cake shop run by a sole trader to a big enterprise manufacturing spare parts with five branches abroad.)

During my years in consultancy I met many entrepreneurs who had failed. They were very skilled and did their jobs well – joiners, bakers, accountants and so on. But they didn't realize one thing: Being an excellent employee doesn't lead to success as an entrepreneur. So pay attention to the following questions, please.

QUESTIONNAIRE

ARE YOU READY TO RIDE TWO HORSES AT THE SAME TIME?

As I have already mentioned, probably the most frequent mistake made by new entrepreneurs is the presumption that being good at one's trade automatically means being a successful entrepreneur. However, doing business without employees means you need to be versatile. You need to be a sales manager and an accountant, a marketing specialist as well as a debt collector. You won't be playing just one role. You will actually be switching roles as required. Are you ready for that?

ARE YOU WILLING TO TAKE RISKS?

Establishing a new company is always linked to a certain level of risk. You need to expect that some things won't work out, at least not the way you planned. On the other hand, if you're not willing to take risks, you won't earn much. Sometimes it is necessary to leave your safe haven and take a leap into the air to find out if you can fly.

Look back at your life and try to remember how you have coped with risks so far, for instance, when signing a lease or when getting a new job. Does the thought of having to take risks unnerve you? If you feel really afraid and uncomfortable about it, you should think twice before you start your business.

CAN YOU MAKE DECISIONS?

Decision making is an inseparable part of business. You will need to decide many things, from trifling issues to those of strategic importance – and then you must stand behind your decisions. If you are hesitant, this could be very problematic for you. You will need to consider the following:

- Will your company do business exclusively online, or will you need to search for non-residential premises for your office or shop?
- Will you need employees?
- Will you focus only on a target group of customers, or will the focus be on something that will appeal to the wider masses?

And then:
- How will you promote your company?
- What sources will you use to fund your company?

And that is just the beginning. Some people are unsettled by merely having to decide which restaurant they should go to for lunch. If you are one of those, pause and consider whether you really want and have the stomach to go through the decision-making process several times a day – where the consequences matter much more than when deciding what to eat for lunch.

ARE YOU FLEXIBLE ENOUGH?

Flexibility is a word frequently used in business. You need to be flexible in terms of your working hours as well as when it comes to your clients' requests and how you manage your company. What works today could become obsolete tomorrow. You are the one who needs to respond to changes and keep pace with ever-changing trends. Are you flexible enough, or do you stick to what you know? By stubbornly denying changes or being unwilling to adjust to new circumstances you will, sooner or later, come to grief, in business and in real life.

CAN YOU GIVE UP ON PERFECTIONISM?

We have certainly heard of artists who were never happy with their work, so they kept retouching it over and over again. It is certainly great to be conscientious and keep your work performance at 150 per cent. However, the world isn't perfect and being a perfectionist becomes an obstacle at a certain point. Incessant polishing of details slows down your productivity, your tasks will start accumulating and you will, sooner or later, be drowning in chaos, then falling into apathy and making mistakes. Learn to put your work down at the right time.

ARE YOU REALISTIC?

In the euphoria, so typical of new entrepreneurs, you may feel that your idea is so unique and brilliant that everyone who hears about it will be flabbergasted. One thing is being enthusiastic about your idea, the other is not losing touch with reality. So, you should not be taken aback when the first year of business yields no exorbitant profit (although I'm not saying it cannot happen). A sober approach, having both feet on the ground and realistic expectations will help you to cope more easily with the ups and downs of your business.

ARE YOU READY FOR INITIAL ZERO PROFIT?

As it's already been said, you need to take into account that you realistically won't be earning much the first year. Ideally, you can rely on other sources of income, reserves in your family finances or your savings, which will allow you to concentrate on your work and overcome the difficult initial period as quickly as possible. Even if you are lucky enough to make money from the very start, you will most likely have to reinvest your profit back into your business in order to keep it growing. But your company will stabilize eventually and your profit will enable you to pay wages and cover your business investment. You just need to understand that it won't happen immediately.

Wu Yajun, boss of the Chinese company Longfor Properties, is the number one female billionaire in China. She earned her $4.5 billion net worth through due diligence. She turns down requests for interviews with a smile: "You see, there's not much I can tell. I'm simply a person who cares about her business." There is no trace of arrogance. According to some insiders, this lady became the richest woman in China thanks to her tireless perfectionism. One of her business partners likes to tell a story that speaks volumes about her. When he visited the Longfor sample house, he left his shoes in front of the door. When he was leaving, he found that somebody had turned his shoes around. The toes were now facing out of the house so that he could put them on more easily. This diligence and care for clients has paid off. According to a recent survey among customers, Longfor is the number one development company. (4)

CAN YOU ACCEPT YOUR OWN MISTAKES?

You'll be doing many things for the first time, so – quite logically – you won't be able to avoid mistakes. Some will be rather small, some big. But even if you put a foot really wrong, it shouldn't discourage you or distract you from your effort to succeed. You should realize that if all entrepreneurs closed down their businesses whenever they made a big mistake, there would be no companies at all!

If you suffer a setback, learn from your mistake and make use of the experience so that you can fare better next time. Take a look at Ben Silbermann. He invented an application called Tote. Have you ever heard of it? Probably not, because it was flop. If Silbermann had given up trying, the world would have never seen Pinterest – which everyone knows about, right?

ARE YOU ABLE TO TAKE CONTROL?

One of the most difficult aspects of business you need to come to grips with is being in control. As the company owner, you need to take the reins and take control over every operation and development in your company. You will need to negotiate with your customers and suppliers; if you have employees, you must tell them what to do; among many other things. You have to be ready to take charge and be the boss. If you have problems with being a leader, it will be extremely hard for you to own and run your company.

And here is one more important note. If you're really determined to run your own business, but you've realized that your mindset could be an obstacle to your success, don't hesitate to change it. Don't believe sceptics who say that nurture cannot win out over nature, that our nature is determined by genes and cannot be altered. Everything can be changed. It only depends on how strong your motivation, will, willingness and patience to work on change is. You can find yourself a coach, choose a suitable personal development course, or at least study the literature available on the topic that troubles you. When the student is ready, a teacher can always be found!

COMBINING WORK AND MOTHERHOOD

Motherhood is a gift you can use for your own development, including your business development. Of course, it is not easy to combine them at the beginning. If you have a small baby at home, or are about to have one, you need to think through how you will combine taking care of business with taking care of your baby. How much support from your partner and people around you can you count on?

Sarah Palin, former Alaskan governor and candidate for US vice-president, returned to her office three days after giving birth to her baby. She came to work with the baby and her husband. Although they could have easily hired a nanny, Sarah took care of the baby with the help of her relatives. The Google vice-president Marissa Mayer started working for Yahoo during the first six months of her pregnancy. She was determined to take only a couple of weeks maternity leave, during which she still planned to work at least part time. But not every woman is like Sarah and Marissa. If you feel inside that running a business while taking care of small children would be too much of a burden, postpone setting up your company until your offspring have grown up a bit. It is better to be a happy mother (and employee) than a businesswoman who is a nervous wreck and thus also an unstable mum.

MAKE USE OF YOUR MATERNITY LEAVE

If you have a baby when your business is already running smoothly, you have no other choice but to continue with the business you've started. Otherwise you could lose everything you've built in a couple of months. However, women typically decide to start up their own business during their maternity leave. Why?

- In countries where companies don't generally like employing mothers and there is not a large pool of flexible jobs, having one's own business is one way a woman with small children can earn sufficient income. The urge to start up a business may also come from a feeling of uncertainty about returning to the original employer.
- Motherhood usually shakes a woman's value system. You discover during this time what it is you actually want to do and what really matters to you.
- Maternity leave is the perfect time to take a look at your current occupation anew and try out, without commitment, what you really like and what interests you.

Businesswomen on maternity leave very often:
- do the work they did before as employees independently (accounting, consulting, sales...);
- are inspired by an idea related to their current situation (private nursery school, mothers club, online shop with children's clothes, healthy lifestyle food, etc.); or
- turn a hobby into a profession (from making marmalades or producing cosmetics at home to restoring furniture, translating, etc.).

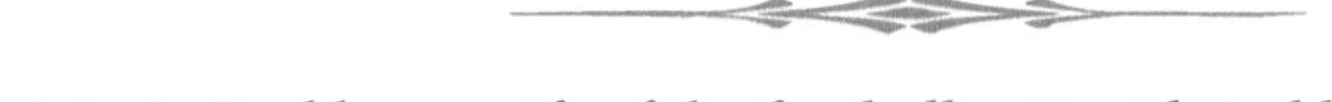

Victoria Beckham, wife of the footballer David Beckham, for a long time was known to the world primarily as a former member of the Spice Girls. But Victoria later became a renowned fashion designer and businesswoman who, in addition to her career, takes care of her three sons and daughter. As she has openly confessed, she finds it hard to work while taking care of her children and husband, who travels a lot. In an interview, she spoke about her daily routine, which starts when Victoria has

the bathroom all to herself for half an hour at 6.30 am. After the children get up and have breakfast, she gets down to work at 8.30 am. Her working hours are until 4 pm. Then she picks up the boys from school and drives them to their after-school activities before spending time with her daughter, who is looked after by a nanny during the day. After doing homework and having dinner, the oldest son finally falls asleep at 9.30 pm, and then the Beckhams have some time for themselves. Victoria gets to bed at around midnight. As you can see, unless you are willing to hand your children over to an army of assistants and not to see them for days, combining work with family life is unavoidable, even if you are a rich and successful celebrity.

GET SOME HELP AND SUPPORT

You may be the most talented businessperson in the world, but you won't get far on your own. Like everybody in business, you need a team. If you want to start up your business while you are still on maternity leave, then you won't manage without one or two other people (partner, nanny, parents, relatives, friends). You should have at least some help with the housework (partner) and a babysitter (nanny) in case you need to go to an important meeting.

KNOW THE VALUE OF YOUR TIME

Running a business takes up more time than regular employment. On the other hand, you are free to decide your own working hours. You can thus adjust your business activities to fit in with your family regime and arrange your working hours so that you can spend time with your family and relax, without disfavouring your customers.

Only 60 per cent of your work activities are planned. The remaining 40 per cent consists of spontaneous and unanticipated activities. Remember this when planning your schedule.

- **Make a list of priorities**
  You need to know which tasks are the most important so that you can spend as much time on them as you need to and complete them without unnecessary stress. Get used to the fact that no one can do everything 100 per cent, and don't worry about it. If you don't hire a cleaning lady, your house won't be spick-and-span. So what? The world certainly won't stop spinning.
- **Write a to do list**
  Jot down any ideas you have about the implementation of the tasks and add the time required for doing them. If there's a big task, split it into smaller parts and make a timetable so that you can do everything in time.
- **Don't overstretch yourself**
  Think realistically about your capabilities and the time you have available. Don't put on your shoulders more weight than they can bear. Delegate everything you can to others and, if it becomes necessary, don't be afraid to say no.
- **Plan the schedule for the next day every evening**
  Plan the most important and difficult tasks for the time of day when you are the most productive.
- **Don't forget to take breaks**
  Everybody has different needs when it comes to rest time. Generally speaking, several shorter breaks are more efficient than a long one.

DON'T FORGET ABOUT YOURSELF

When combining business with caring for your kids, don't forget about yourself and your needs. Treat yourself to a small pleasure every day. Take a walk in the fresh air, buy a small bouquet of violets or call a friend. Relax, do some exercise, spoil yourself with a massage or a hot bubble bath. And praise yourself for everything you did well!

Don't neglect your hobbies. They will help you take your mind off everyday worries and the time you dedicate to your children will be of much better quality, even though there will be less of it. This will then be reflected in your business.

A mother with two small children and a start-up company may find the suggestion of relaxing for half an hour in a bath tub absurd, but if you want to stay healthy, keeping your foot down on the accelerator in the weeks, months and years to come, you will need to change your view.

CHERISH YOUR RELATIONSHIP

Give enough care and attention to your partner – so that they remain your partner and soul mate and don't become just a nanny, a walking credit card or the one who constantly keeps asking for something from you that you have no time or mood for (e.g. attention, sex, a weekend break). Home should remain a safe place for you, your partner and your children, a place you like to return to and where you build up the energy necessary for the "outside world".

Now you have an idea about what it takes to be an entrepreneur. I didn't mean to discourage or scare you, just to help you get grounded and show you what's coming.

QUESTIONS TO CONSIDER

 **AM I SUITED TO BUSINESS?**

Now you should be able to give a clear answer to this question. If you don't feel up to business at the moment, try to work a little harder on your mindset or choose a different path. There is no shame or loss in not having your own business. There are many ways in which you can achieve self-fulfilment – you will certainly find the right one for you.

AM I READY TO TAKE CHARGE?

Decision making is an inseparable part of business. If you hire employees, you are assuming responsibility for them, while being able to come to agreements with them too. If you can understand what taking charge means, you'll find it comes easily.

AM I AWARE THAT MY IDEAS WON'T ALL MATERIALIZE AT ONCE?

New entrepreneurs need to deal with the fact that it usually takes a while before they start making profit.

AM I READY TO COPE WITH FAILURES?

I don't mean you should think about doing badly in the future. It is just fine if you realize that you don't necessarily need to be successful all the time and don't let failure bring you down.

DO I KNOW HOW TO COMBINE BUSINESS WITH MOTHERHOOD?

Do you know to what extent the people around you are willing and ready to help when you start up your business?

Chapter 3

Incubators are not just for babies

Let your business idea ripen

You have decided to start up your own business, and now it's time to think about what exactly you want to do and what kind of company you will establish. Your head is probably full of questions: Where shall I begin? What shall I do first? What mustn't I forget? All of these questions are absolutely relevant and they are asked by every new entrepreneur. They certainly shouldn't put you off your intent.

Before you start focusing on your company, you first need to focus on yourself. Your business must be something that will really interest you. In other words, if you hate working out and avoid it like the plague, then the last thing you should consider is running a fitness centre. You should keep in mind that establishing and running your new business will take up a great deal of your time. If you hate what you're doing (even if it is profitable and hired instructors would actually handle the exercise classes), you won't feel connected and will probably give it up pretty quickly. So, focus on something you like and find interesting instead. Results will come sooner and you will have an internal feeling of satisfaction. That's why this is certainly worth thinking carefully about.

HOW TO FIGURE OUT WHAT YOU WOULD ENJOY DOING

Think about yourself and what kind of business activities attract you. Naturally, you will hardly make a success of a new pharmacy when there are already three within a kilometre. A shop selling luxury furniture probably won't be the best choice if you live in a poor region with a high unemployment rate. It is crucial to figure out what other people, meaning your potential clients, will be interested in, but we will discuss external circumstances later on. At this point it would only confuse you as you are trying to figure out what you actually want.

STAGE 1

Take a pencil and paper and do a small exercise. Clear your head and write down without hesitation everything that comes to your mind regarding the business orientation of your future company and what you personally like. You may have ideas about how you could improve something in your environment. Some of these ideas could be used for starting up your business and be your competitive advantage if you do things differently. Don't be shy, jot down everything that enters your mind. You can get started by asking yourself these simple questions:

- What are my hobbies and free time activities?
- Do I have any special interests?
- Is there anything I would like to solve or get involved in?
- What are my capabilities and talents?
- What do I have experience with?
- Is there anything I could do for the rest of my life?
- What would I like to change in my surroundings?
- What do I dislike or feel is missing from shops or services?

Done? If you get some other ideas later on, write them down, but you can put your notes aside for the time being and give yourself a little break. Now, when you have looked critically at your notes, you may have got a little scared. What may seem crazy at first glance is certainly not extravagant from the perspective of your soul. Hot-air balloons, good food, gardening, riding motorbikes, teaching Spanish, horses, furniture restoration, books... Did you put down that pharmacy of yours? If you did, that's good, because even if the idea is not viable, it will lead you to alternatives. What about herbs, remedial therapy, health massage, Ayurveda, yoga, etc.? This is actually what the second stage is about.

STAGE 2

Pick from the list all the items you find interesting and you think could work as a business. Being fond of riding motorbikes could lead you to establishing a courier service. Good food may transform into a catering company. And gardening? You've mentioned books, so why not try to write manuals with tips for gardeners or set up a blog about gardening? Or you can sew hand-made gardening aprons. There are many possibilities. You don't have to restrict yourself to proven ideas, something that has already been done by somebody else. You can focus on something nobody offers, something that fills a gap in the market, or on something they're doing completely wrong in the corner shop that drives you nuts because you would do it better/differently.

A nice example is the "Dog Detective". Klára Carbová's dog Jack got lost when she and her husband were walking him in the forest. They searched for Jack for many hours and at that moment they would have given anything for somebody to help them with their search. They eventually found the dog and this experience led them to found an agency that looks for lost dogs (5).

Zoe Cole often struggled to find child-friendly hotels within the UK that would offer the same high standards and facilities as romantic or boutique weekends away. She also found that there were very few places online to go to find these kinds of hotels. So, she came up with Crisp White Sheets to fill this gap. The company works with unique, quirky and high end hotels that are also child friendly. (6)

THINK ABOUT YOUR BUSINESS GOALS

In order to be successful, you need to know why you want to enter the world of business. Try to make a list of the goals you would like to achieve by answering the following questions:

- Why am I starting a business?
- Do I want to boost my current income, or is this something I really want to do with my life?
- What do I want to achieve with my business? (Do I want to expand abroad or stick with a small family company, etc.?)
- Where do I see myself in five years' time? And in ten years' time?
- Do I want to build a company I can pass on to my children one day?

It is important to know what you want to achieve in life. Some people only see their business activity as a hobby. If you are one of those, be careful. You won't take working for your company seriously and, if you don't invest the necessary effort and money, it can easily happen that sooner or later you will go bankrupt or have to subsidise the business with your savings, which is wrong.

Of course, it is possible for your company to also be your hobby, but on the condition that you are passionate about the subject.

Think about what you want to achieve in your life in the years to come. If you are young, newly married and planning to have a baby, you should set your business intentions accordingly. You have to anticipate that, unless you want your child to be taken care of by your partner, nanny or a relative, the baby will occupy a great deal of your time and attention. We are all different and each of us has a different attitude to life and motherhood, but it is certainly a good idea to reserve rather more time for our non-working duties. So, if you are planning to build a company that will require you to work eighty hours a week with no holidays, you should also take into account the needs of your family and the people around you.

Without a thorough understanding of your life and personal targets, there's no point in thinking about your business intent. You know how it is: Plans are made, but life changes.

NIGHT CLUBS ARE NOT FOR EARLY BIRDS

In the previous chapter I compared business to parenthood. A company is a commitment, just like a baby. You cannot simply run away back to your previous life if you are not in the right mood or having a bad hair day. Your previous life no longer exists. The way you spend your free time, whether you have any at all, social contacts, the money you have, everything is completely different now.

Take a look at your lifestyle from the perspective of choosing the ideal type of business. If you are an early bird, you certainly don't want to open a night club, whereas a "night owl" won't open a bakery. When running a leisure facility for adults (such as a language or dancing school and the like) you need to anticipate that most of your work will take place after the usual working hours of others. Becoming a representative of a foreign brand requires frequent business trips. Unless your business is exclusively online, you should also consider the distance between your company address (brick-and-mortar shop, workshop, centre, etc.) and potential customers. The Internet and social networks are powerful tools, but not complete salvation.

WHICH FIELDS HAVE REAL POTENTIAL?

Listed below are a range of sectors in which your business can operate. (Later on, we will also look into how you can determine the viability of your intent.):
- Handmade goods
- Applied arts (design, photographs, illustrations...)
- Web design
- Online business
- Mail order services
- Antiques
- Graphic design
- Private tutoring, remedial classes
- Child care and family services
- Pet care
- Consultancy (legal, financial...)
- Consultant, trainer, coach (nutrition, fitness, personal development...)
- Health, beauty and wellness services
- Cleaning services

- Wholesale
- Gastronomy and catering
- Manufacture and sale of (natural) cosmetics

Notice that this list contains mostly services and businesses with added value. Successful businesses often stem from a hobby, but not every hobby automatically implies you will have a reliable source of income. Just remember how many writers there are who are passionate about writing and dedicate all their time to it but often, despite their books being popular, don't earn a living and therefore cannot afford to leave their job (often working as editors in publishing houses, translators, creative artists in advertising agencies, etc.). On the other hand, it is true that blogging, which has become so popular, has for quite a few led to a successful business.

Therefore, you should decide if your hobby has the potential to become your future business, and if not, which way it needs to go in order to yield profit. (You know every plant and animal far and wide, so why don't you offer trips or camps for children?)

PICK A FITTING BUSINESS MODEL

In addition to the line of business, you also need to choose the business model that best suits your ideas. Let's have a look at the most common ones.

DROPSHIPPING

You can make use of this US business model if you want to do business online and you don't have funds for the initial start-up, labour force and sufficient storage space. By becoming a retailer, you sell goods from a third-party wholesaler or manufacturer. You present the goods as your own, although, in fact, you don't come in contact with them. Not until a product is sold do you then buy it from the third party and have it shipped directly to the customer.

Dropshipping may be a suitable model for women on maternity leave or small entrepreneurs and is most often used by e-shops.

Negatives: If your customer cancels the order or sends the goods back to you, you won't get your costs back, since you are the one who bought the goods and they belong to you. Make sure you choose a trustworthy supplier. If you don't stock the products you sell and you never hold them in your hands, it may be risky to guarantee their quality.

FRANCHISE

A franchise allows you to do business without any other previous experience or much capital (depending on the franchise model), and thus without big risk. All you need to do is to buy a licence from a company that offers franchising, hence acquiring the right to use the trademark, know-how and all necessary support including training and even marketing support.

Negatives: The "tax" for having a developed business recipe fall into your lap can take the form of frequent controls carried out by the licence owner to maintain a certain level of brand and product quality. In addition to the initial purchase price of the licence, you have to assume that you will need to pay a regular (monthly) fee for the licence or make contributions to the marketing fund. Also, you won't be allowed to sell anything else in your shop. Most McDonald's are franchises and you cannot buy a hot dog there.

MULTI-LEVEL MARKETING (MLM)

Multi-level marketing (MLM), or network marketing, is suitable if you don't have your own marketing ideas or initial capital but you still want to decide your earnings and keep improving your skills. As a seller, not only do you get remuneration for the products you sell, but you also receive a share of sales achieved by other people. MLM can be seen as a kind of initial stage of your independent business.

This business model is quite widespread in some countries. Probably all of us have at least once met a representative from Mary Kay, Avon, or Kleeneze, three of the most famous MLM companies that have been active in the market for many years doing their business absolutely legally and transparently.

The hint of controversy associated with MLM is due to the fact it can be easily mistaken for fraudulent "pyramid schemes". However, MLM is different. While pyramid schemes don't create any added value, as they trade with worthless vouchers or subscriptions to various courses, in MLM there is always a real product.

Negatives: The biggest risk lies in choosing the company whose products you want to sell and in differentiating between pyramid schemes and MLM companies. You should also be prepared to exert great effort, diligence and determination if you want to achieve decent earnings.

SOCIAL BUSINESS

Simply put, a social business is one that is beneficial to society, often opening up job opportunities for people with disabilities. It could be a massage salon, café, cleaning service, garden centre, it is up to you. As the owner of a social company (whatever its legal form is) you'll probably use the profit for further development, and the money required for the busi-ness can often come from grants or donations.

Negatives: Being a social entrepreneur will probably make it more difficult for you to access the most common methods of financing (traditional bank loans, etc.). Moreover, your de-termination to follow ethical principles may be your competi-tive disadvantage. And, if you employ people who are disad-vantaged on the labour market, you will first probably need to overcome any initial doubts your customers may have.

The suitable legal forms for your company will be discussed in Chapter 9, which focuses on the legal aspects of business, so I will only make a brief comment on this here.

You may be attracted to an activity that you presume is not suit-able for traditional business and would be much better off in the non-profit sector. The fact is that the word "non-profit" is a rather confusing term, because a non-profit organization, although its primary intention is something other than making profit, must still follow the rules of the market. If it doesn't function as a commer-cial company, it won't survive. Getting funds for the activities of any non-profit organization, whether from grants or from corporate or private donors, is no easy task and it requires business skills in-cluding marketing, public relations (PR) and often also networking.

Mary Kay founded her company of the same name when she was forty-five. She founded it with the intention of creating work opportunities for women, which was an unprecedented thing in the US at that time. A com-pany where women could actualize and earn according to the effort they exerted. Mary Kay became a pioneer in female entrepreneurship and she

succeeded in building one of the biggest companies in the world in its field. Nowadays, the company operates in more than thirty countries and has hundreds of thousands of women consultants.

TWO IS BETTER THAN ONE – OR MAYBE NOT?

The first inkling to start a business often originates in a sandpit or in a day care centre. Women often found their own companies when they are on maternity leave (and sometimes they are left with no other choice; for example, if the labour market in their country discriminates against mothers with small children), and they enjoy starting a new adventure in pairs. They also know that with a new baby to take care of they won't be available to their clients non-stop. Therefore, it is advantageous to start up a business as a partnership and, if need be, one can substitute for the other.

However, it is not just about practical advantages. It is nice when you don't do everything by yourself and you can share your ideas and problems with someone who has a common interest. You may have doubts that the idea to enlarge your café by adding an outdoor terrace will attract enough new clients, but if your friend and business partner is enthusiastic about it, there is probably something in it. Or you may be facing hard times: Your child has just started school, your partner has problems at work, you are tired or you are in a bad mood because you sent out the wrong invoices a while ago. Who will be your emotional support, encouraging you to believe these problems are just temporary and everything will soon be fine again? Your business partner!

As usual, in addition to all the great advantages of running a business in twos, there are also many risks lurking in such a scenario – and these can destroy both your business and your friendship. If you know about them in advance and prepare for them, you can easily avoid them

START A BUSINESS WITH A PERSON YOU KNOW WELL

You meet at the hairdresser's and you always have a nice chat about books. Liking someone and sharing the same interests is great, but it is not enough for running a successful business together.

When you were children you were best friends, you just haven't seen each other for the past twenty years. Your childhood friend may be a great person, but before you step into business shoulder to shoulder, get to know more about her – how she's living now, what her life situation and values are, what she likes, what she expects from life and so on.

You may be birds of a feather because you are in the same life situation. Fine, but isn't your mutual understanding only due to the fact that you are both divorced, have children of similar ages and are thus facing similar trouble? Will you still nod in agreement in a year or two?

You have been colleagues for several years. Knowing each other's work habits is great; many women who start businesses on the basis of personal relationships initially lack this insight. The risk is that despite having grandiose plans, your friend may prove to be a lazy sloth, or your responsible colleague may turn into a nit-picking tyrant before your eyes. Again, you can prevent this by talking to each other and discussing all the possible risks.

EXPLAIN TO EACH OTHER WHY YOU WANT TO DO BUSINESS

We've discussed business goals in this chapter, so you know that two people can hardly agree with each other over the long term if one of them sees the business as a source of financing for her adventurous travels around the world, while for the other one it is a matter of the heart.

SET THE RULES

The more precisely and earlier you can state them, the better. It is not about having your office walls plastered with lists of dos and don'ts, but you should know what you can expect from each other and how much time each of you are willing to dedicate to work with respect to your life situations. What seems reasonable during a friendly chat over dessert in a cake shop may be a problem in business. A systematic mother of adult children who prefers a consistent and calm working pace may have different opinions on how a company should work than an irritable mother of three-year-old twins who is used to working in fits and starts and making decisions impulsively.

DON'T UNDERESTIMATE CONTRACTS

You should see contracts as a matter of fact, not as a manifestation of mistrust. Sure, your business partner is your best friend and she would never deceive you. All the more reason why she shouldn't have a problem and should agree with putting things on paper. This protects both of you.

DISCUSS ONLY BUSINESS IN THE OFFICE

You can, of course, give your friend the joyful news and tell her your partner finally booked a family holiday to Mallorca. But don't mistake the office for a café; plan to talk about private matters after work. It works the other way around too. When you are in a café or playing squash, try to avoid discussing business, if possible. Mental hygiene is important and business is no ladies' club. To make it work, hold regular meetings, divide your tasks, set deadlines and make reports.

DIVIDE YOUR COMPETENCES

It is important to agree beforehand what each of you will be in charge of and responsible for. Otherwise, you risk that the company will be floundering like a boat without a helmsman or that you will be like two roosters in a fighting arena.

BE PREPARED TO COMPROMISE

Even though you might be soul mates, you will certainly be surprised how many times you may differ in business. Learn how you can come to agreements. Sometimes give in and accept a compromise. Always search for what is connecting you, not dividing you. You'll find a solution that is satisfactory for both parties much more easily.

BE OPEN

If your friend is driving you crazy or some business matter makes you angry, don't keep it to yourself. Talk about it. Don't let problems and disputes pile up. Solve them in a timely manner. Otherwise, the volcano will erupt and cover you in lava. Don't reproach each other for mistakes, because all of us make them.

Almost identical rules apply if you run a business with your life partner or husband. The difference is that an intimate relationship and business are an even more fragile and explosive combination, so it is twice as advisable to follow the principles you have agreed upon. Few marriages can actually handle the bankruptcy of a family business, and very few companies can survive the break-up of a marriage. So that you don't have to suffer for your partner's mistakes for the rest of your life, I recommend that you study carefully the legal provisions concerning joint business ventures between married couples.

QUESTIONS TO CONSIDER

DO I HAVE A CLEAR IDEA ABOUT WHAT I LIKE DOING?

It is the impulse to go back to the list you made that helps you formulate your business plan.

WHAT IS MY BUSINESS PLAN?

Write it down. You must be clear about whether you're going to sell a product or a service and what kind of product or service it will be. Don't be afraid, even if you have several ideas at the moment.

HOW WILL BUSINESS FIT INTO MY LIFE?

It is an important question, because if your business is not in line with your lifestyle, you can certainly expect problems in the future.

WILL I ENJOY DOING THIS WORK EVEN AFTER MANY YEARS?

You don't want to find out after a couple of years to your disillusionment that you've invested a lot of time and effort into something that no longer interests you. There's no way you can completely eliminate this risk, of course, as life likes to lead us along winding paths, but accepting a challenge and succumbing to momentary flights of fancy are two different things. That's why this question requires careful consideration and thought.

Chapter 4
Meet your customer!
Give them everything they want

However your idea came into being, it is obvious that you've fallen in love with it. But before you turn it into your business, you need to make sure it is viable. It is nice that you can sew fifty cute plush toys per week, but if they remain in a cupboard in your home, they won't earn you your bread and butter. You don't want to waste time on something that won't yield profit, however much you may like it.

So, let's focus on the processes that will help you determine the viability of your idea. This is the moment when you need to start taking your business really seriously. Are you ready to roll up your sleeves and get down to it? Alright, let's go...

WHO'S THAT? YOUR CLIENT!

The time has come to ask yourself a couple of questions that are not about you, but about your environment. The customer and the market – these are the keywords you need to focus on now. The better the evaluation of your potential market, the more qualified decisions you'll be able to take for your company.

 **WHO IS THE TARGET MARKET?**

Whether you plan on opening a pet food shop or you intend to run a beauty parlour, you need to find out whether there are enough people who would be interested in buying your goods or services.

It is logical that you want to spread the word about your company to as many people as possible, but also consider how many people will be interested in your product or service and how many people will actually buy it. That's why it is important to define your target market very precisely. When you then focus on that target market, selling will be much more efficient.

The size of your target market will reveal to what extent your hobby is practically usable for business. Your hobby may be something you like, but at the same time something that appeals to just a few people in your region or country. It is a good idea to check up on this information early on, as it will allow you to rethink whether you can extend or reasonably transform your idea into something similar that will appeal to a wider public. If you intend to provide translation and interpretation services from an exotic language, consider offering language courses and guided tours, importing interesting or traditional goods from that country, and so on. The Internet will certainly help you, and you will quickly find who has had a similar idea and when. Judging on the response to the previous project, you can estimate how many people were interested and thus get a picture of how big your relevant customer base is (in marketing research these are so-called secondary data).

"My life has always been about music. I've played the guitar and piano since I was a small child, and I've also sung. But already in my teenage years I came to understand that I didn't have what it takes for a solo career, and after I finished my studies, I became a teacher at a music school. Once a friend of mine needed to sell his expensive guitar in a hurry and asked me if I could help. I found him a buyer and negotiated a very good price. I don't know how it happened, but soon there were other people asking me for help. I realized I liked doing these deals. After a while it occurred to me that I could open my own shop with musical instruments, but I knew I had no chance to succeed in the small town where I lived. So, in order to make my dream come true, I changed my life completely and moved to London. And I must say I've never regretted it."

(Alice, 41, USA)

WHAT DOES YOUR PERFECT CUSTOMER LOOK LIKE?

Another thing you need to do is to make a profile of your ideal customer. It is not enough to just come up with a general definition like "my ideal customer is a middle-aged person". You need to describe the person in great detail. Before you can do that, you need two types of information: demographic and psychographic.

1. Demographic:
- Age
- Town/City
- Sex
- Personal situation (parent, teenager, retired, etc.)
- Marital status
- Income

This is the first type of background information you need to compile a customer profile. However, there's much more you need to take into account.

2. Psychographic:

This is information on aspects of the client's personality, including:

- Interests
- Attitudes
- Behaviour
- Lifestyle

Both demographic and psychographic information are essential for making a realistic profile. Demographic information will help you determine the type of person who will buy your goods or services. Psychographic information goes one step further and shows you why the potential client will buy from you.

To facilitate making the profile, imagine that your client and your company are entering into a partnership. Describe exactly, and in the greatest detail possible, what your business partner should be like. For example, a man or woman who comes to buy your goat's cheese or orders a web design. Put their characteristics down on paper. Close your eyes and imagine that the ideal client of your "artful hands" shop is standing right in front of you. The person may look like this:

My ideal client is a woman aged between twenty-five and thirty-five. She is from a middle or lower-middle income group and the mother of a new born baby or a small child. She is creative, good with her hands and likes making decorative things in her free time. However, she has a busy lifestyle and she doesn't have the time to make everything from scratch, which is why she needs kits or sets that will make it easier to get started.

And what is your customer like? Take a pencil and paper and describe him or her.

WHAT DOES YOUR CUSTOMER REALLY NEED?

Find out if your goods or services really satisfy a certain need. Take a look at the characteristics of your ideal customer and think about the following:

- What does your customer need for life?
- What is that person missing?
- What is he or she searching for?
- Can I offer that individual something that meets their needs?
- Can I offer something that he or she needs but doesn't have access to?

Many companies only concentrate on what customers want, and they forget that a company with long-term goals should focus first on clients' needs and then on their wishes. This may at first seem to be just word-splitting, but it is not. True, people buy things they want all the time, but it is much more likely they will buy things they really need. Especially when they have to dig deep into their pockets. You know it yourself: Charity begins at home.

Now, when you've made the profile of your ideal client and know your target market, you can compare your findings with the goods or services you intend to sell. If they fail to satisfy your customer's needs, you have two options – either you re-assess your ideal customer or your offer.

WHAT DOES THE CUSTOMER WANT?

Of course, it is not off-topic to consider what the client craves. A wish is not as important as a need, but it still influences an individual's decisions on purchases. Most of us buy primarily what we need, but if we can choose from more than just one product, we pick the one we desire. You certainly need a winter coat, but why should you buy a grey one when there's a trendy red one with a hood? People are often much more willing to pay a higher price for something they want than for something they only need.

Look at it from this perspective: You and your competition offer the same product but with different features. Your competitor focuses on merely satisfying the need and offers a product in a stripped-down version, which is enough to meet customers' needs. You, by contrast, have taken into account the need AND the desire, so your product offers, in addition to the necessary functions, some other features customers long for. Where do you think these customers will do their shopping? In your shop, naturally!

What exactly does the customer's "I want" mean? What does he or she want? Think about the following questions:

- What makes the customer feel good?
- What arouses his or her emotions?
- What helps that individual feel beautiful?
- What does he or she consider beautiful?
- What do they like?
- Does your customer want to be any different?
- What about ecological, organic and environmental concerns?

When you join your ideal customer's desires with their needs, can you imagine how your goods or services fit in? If you can, your thoughts are going in the right direction.

"I was looking forward to opening my own shop so much. I went for a haberdashery as I knew that all the shops in the neighbourhood selling these kinds of goods had ceased, and many people had no idea where they could buy thread, buttons or wool anymore. Every night before falling asleep, I vividly imagined who my customers would be. And I saw people coming to my shop, young mums who wanted to crochet a sweater or make a furry teddy bear for their children, elderly women who mended clothes for the whole family, and girls who had forgotten to take some wool from home for their handicraft lesson. I pictured them in the greatest detail, with expressions on their faces, what they were saying, what they were wearing and where they were going, if they worked or studied and how they spent their leisure time. I actually had no idea that this is what handbooks on entrepreneurship recommend. I simply enjoyed spontaneously viewing this in front of my eyes."
(Louise, 34, UK)

FIND A GAP IN THE MARKET

A gap in the market represents one specific and unique group of people who may be attracted to your business. Even though you can start up a company that doesn't fill any gap or satisfy the needs of a wide public, for you as a new entrepreneur it would probably be biting off more than you can chew. So, it is much better if you first find a "blank spot on the map" that you can fill with your offer.

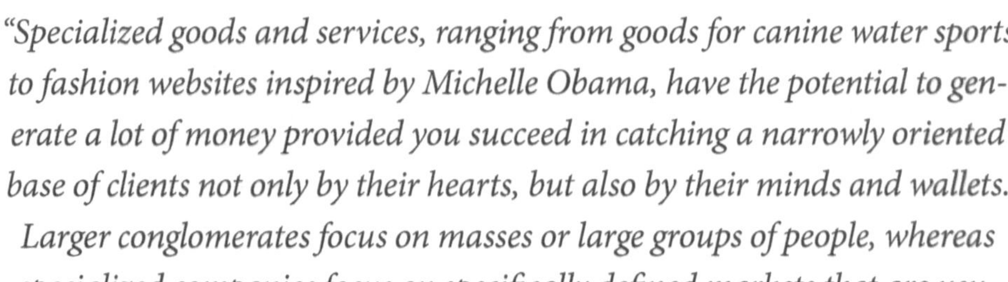

"Specialized goods and services, ranging from goods for canine water sports to fashion websites inspired by Michelle Obama, have the potential to generate a lot of money provided you succeed in catching a narrowly oriented base of clients not only by their hearts, but also by their minds and wallets. Larger conglomerates focus on masses or large groups of people, whereas specialized companies focus on specifically defined markets that are usually overlooked by big competitors, insufficiently supplied or perceived as marginal." (7)

There's the space for you! By filling a gap in the market your company will gain the hallmark of uniqueness, which will help you stand out from the competition. But remain realistic! Although it is nice to fill a gap in the market, if you only have a couple of customers, there's probably no point in being unique. There will be a certain group of people who will only be attracted to you, but how do you discover them? Consider some of the following circumstances.

WHAT IS CURRENTLY IN?

Be the first one to take interest into account. Your product or service doesn't have to be popular all around the world. It is just fine if your ideal customer identifies with it.

It is easy to have a look around the market and find out what customers pay most attention to. You will only discover whether the best-selling products are handmade jewellery or hot air balloon flying courses with the help of media and social networks. You can learn a lot from thematic catalogues and websites – including those crowd-funding ones where you can see what projects people most often try to get money for and what the public response is.

But this is only the first step, since the mere fact that something is popular doesn't automatically mean there is a gap in the market for a specialized product.

WHAT IS NECESSARY BUT LACKING?

In some areas the market is so oversaturated with ideas and products that there's not an inch of space. Quite the contrary, there can also be a "saturation" of offers. If you decide you want to try to squeeze in, you should realize how exhausting this fight will be. In fact, there may be more beautiful handmade mobile covers, like those you are producing with such verve, than mobile phones on the market. You'd better accept the fact that the market is oversaturated with this type of offer. Again, I can only advise one thing: Try to make your offer unique and adjust it to meet demand. (Remember, for instance, the example with the pharmacy. Do you have a different, more substantial idea how you could materialize your interest in health into a business?)

On the other hand, a gap in the market is not constant or even fixed. Do you remember the time when so-called flip phones were so popular? This type of phone was, in comparison with what was on offer at the time, something very original. Then came smart phones, and the gap shifted elsewhere. People found something new they wanted and needed – no longer a flip phone, but a smart phone. If you have discovered such a gap in the market, make sure it makes sense and provides you with space for further growth and development.

COMPETITIVE ADVANTAGE

If you have not identified a gap in the market, but you are still determined to do business in that industry, nothing is lost. Make sure your product is unique in some way and differs from the competition, meaning it offers a competitive advantage. It can be the location of your shop, low or – quite the opposite – high price, or an individual approach to your clients.

Many new entrepreneurs make the mistake of running a business in an industry that is oversaturated (which means they found no gap in the market) without offering any competitive advantage.

"I've always wanted to have a newsstand and be in everyday contact with people. The problem was that in the town where I live there are a lot of newsstands. I almost gave up on my dream, but fate had other ideas. A space freed up in a shopping mall. I didn't hesitate and a month later I was the manager of a newsstand. My competitive advantage is the location, which is nearby the main entrance and close to a subway station."

(Monica, 34, USA)

HOW MUCH IS IT GOING TO COST?

Now is the time to set the price at which you are going to sell your goods or services. In principle, we can say that the right price is the price that brings you profit and is acceptable for your customers. But how can we determine that?

Determining the right price can determine whether your business succeeds or fails. There are several methods for setting the right price. You will set your price differently if you bake biscuits or if you run an online tax consulting service. We'll now take a look at the most frequently used price-setting methods.

PRICE BASED ON COSTS

Include in your selling price all the costs incurred: direct (that is production costs such as materials, processing, packaging, distribution, complaints, marketing and promotion) and indirect (rent for office and manufacturing space, utilities, employee salaries, telephones, leasing, fuel, taxes and fees, insurance), plus a reasonable profit margin.

You can use this method, for instance, when you intend to bake the above-mentioned biscuits. After summing up all these costs and adding your mark-up you get the price of the product.

PRICE BASED ON VALUE

The price should be set according to the value the customer thinks is appropriate for a given product or service.

For instance, an accountant (or a consultant or lawyer, for example) doesn't have any manufacturing or distribution costs and their indirect costs are significantly lower in comparison with a manufacturing company. However, the value of the labour is high, and it is perceived as such by the market.

PRICE BASED ON COMPETITION

Find what price similar competitive products are sold for and determine your price after comparing them with the quality of your product. It can be a little higher or lower. However, I only recommend using this pricing method as complementary.

Do you want to open a children's clothing shop? In that case, probably the easiest place to start will be to look around at your competitors. To determine the right price for each product, I recommend using a combination of the above-stated methods. Count up all the costs: direct and indirect + your margin. Compare the final sum with your competition's price. Then do some research on the interest of your age group in the product you offer. I recommend taking your time with this step because if people are not able or willing to pay you the set price, you will not make any money.

A very frequent mistake made by entrepreneurs is that they set the price of their product far too low thinking they will attract more customers. However, the opposite is often the case. Many people are happy to pay extra money because a higher price suggests better quality. Sometimes entrepreneurs attract customers with a low price (that often doesn't even cover the costs) but, the moment they feel they are established on the market, they increase their price. Immediately their customers leave, as they are not willing to pay the higher price. You should thus make sure that the quality and price you offer are well balanced.

Consider how much money your client has for spending or investing. Learn how to distinguish between a product price and the purchasing power of your target market. As we've mentioned before, a wish is something very different from a need!

So, you must determine what prices will safeguard the successful operation of your company, while not being an issue for your ideal customer. Think of the future. Don't offer just one product, but preferably a range of products. Grade the product prices to correspond with different income brackets, just as cosmetic companies do when they offer cheaper products alongside more luxurious brands. Diversify effectively, not only with regard to possible economic recessions, but also to protect you against future competition that might not be there at the moment, but may be there tomorrow.

Now you should know what your company will look like and who your customers will be, what types of goods or services you'll be selling and for what prices.

Now you have to take the last step towards getting your business ready: testing! You know who you should offer your product to and what your competitive advantage is. All you need to do now is to test your product. Make some specimens and hand them out to the people in your area who fit into your target market. What are their reactions to your product? Do they like it as it is, or would they be happier if you modified it? Think about it. The response of your potential customers may generate ideas about how to adjust the product so that it makes its way onto the market more easily.

Testing before you actually start up your business may also save you a lot of money.

QUESTIONS TO CONSIDER

DO I HAVE AN EXACT IDEA ABOUT MY PERFECT CUSTOMER? CAN I DESCRIBE THIS CUSTOMER IN DETAIL?

Remember this is crucial for your business!

DO I KNOW WHICH WISH OR DESIRE MY PRODUCT OR SERVICE IS GOING TO SATISFY?

Your business must fulfil at least your customers' needs, but preferably also their wishes.

WHICH GAP IN THE MARKET WILL I FILL?

Find out to what extent your product satisfies the demand on the market.

IS THERE A GAP FOR MY PRODUCT IN THE MARKET?

Are you certain that nobody else is offering the same goods or services and that they are actually missing from the market? It is important to be absolutely positive about it!

HAVE I TESTED MY PRODUCT? WHAT ARE THE RESPONSES?

Make this very clear before you change anything about your product.

Chapter 5

Remember to pack a compass

Why it is important to have your business plan to hand

You may be asking yourself why you should waste time writing up a tedious document when you know exactly what you want to do and who for and, moreover, you only intend to establish a small company.

Believe it or not, it is really important to formulate a business plan. You're also doing this for those who will be involved in your business in the future. Although your idea is clear to you at the moment, that can easily change when you take further practical steps and when you are confronted with everyone else's opinions as you certainly will be as an entrepreneur.

For one thing, a business plan on paper will show your clear vision to others, and for another, it will serve as your compass. It will help you to hold your course so that you can navigate through the haze of doubts and confusion until you see your goal on the horizon again. It is a necessary tool when you travel through an unknown land – and doing business certainly is an exotic journey, no matter if we are talking about importing wine or manufacturing china.

"A business plan is a written description of the future of your business. A document that illustrates your intent and notion of how it should be implemented. If you scribble it down on the back side of an envelope, you've just written up your business plan, or at least made a start. A business plan will serve its author in many ways. It can be used when you are explaining your vision to potential investors. It may also come in handy for companies trying to attract key employees, searching for new business opportunities, negotiating with suppliers or simply wanting to understand how the company could be managed in a better way." (8)

PERSONAL NAVIGATION AND A TOOL OF PERSUASION

You probably see now that you cannot do without a business plan, at the start or later on, and that you may be reaching for it more often than you would have thought. What can this document help you with?

YOU'LL AVOID MISTAKES

On your journey to success you'll come across many obstacles and you'll be making mistakes. You may go astray, hit a dead end or start building the company in a manner that is predestined to fail. Taking a detailed look at your business plan will tell you if you're acting in accordance with it, keep you on track, and help you avoid fatal mistakes that would require a lot of time, effort and money to rectify.

YOU WON'T SUCCUMB TO EMOTIONS

When you start running your business you will be full of emotions, ranging from initial excitement and euphoria, to staggering fear, apathy and exhaustion.

As soon as you are buried by a wave of emotions that blurs your judgement, you can use your business plan as a compass to help you get back on the right path and get an objective view of things around you.

YOUR TEAM WILL HOLD THE COURSE

You may be starting up a business with another person or you plan to have employees. In any case, you need to make sure that everyone involved knows exactly which direction your company should be heading. Having a business plan will help you.

YOU WILL HAVE A GAME PLAN

As a new company, you need a clear plan laying out what to do now and what to do in the future.

Imagine you're playing a fairy-tale themed board game. There are two pathways open to you: one leading to a prince and the other to a dragon. Your job is to guide your piece to the prince, so you take the path that leads to him. A business plan works in a similar way – it shows you where to go.

YOU WILL CONVINCE INVESTORS MORE EASILY

If you need to borrow money to get started and you are new to the world of business with no experience or track record, it will be easier for you to get financing if you present potential investors with a clear and comprehensible plan of anticipated activities.

*"A friend of mine in Paris is a great promoter of natural cosmetics.
I started to share her enthusiasm after using lotions without chemical
substances which got rid of red patches and spots on my face within a
couple of weeks. 'What if you start importing products of this brand to
your country? You wouldn't need to travel in person for those you need',
she proposed once when I went to see her. At first I was taken aback by
the idea, but then I said to myself – I have worked for ten years in foreign
trade and I can speak French, so why not?*

*Negotiations with the company were surprisingly smooth and the cosmet-
ics sell much better than I had expected. But I feel it is not enough to sell
only via an e-shop and brick-and-mortar shop, and I'm thinking of other
ways I could promote the brand. I'm considering offering the products to
hotels where they provide beauty services, or even setting up a network of
my own cosmetic salons. It's not easy to think everything over carefully, so
I hope I make the right decision."*

(Ella, 38, Germany)

WHEN YOU HAVE A PLAN, NOTHING WILL SURPRISE YOU!

If you take the trouble to formulate your business plan, your company will profit from five advantages. Once you read what they
are, you'll easily understand why it is so important to be guided in
business by a precisely defined plan.

FEASIBILITY

Your idea may sound great and look perfect on paper, but you won't know if it is viable until you start implementing it. A business plan will tell you what your chances are – it includes all the important initial information such as a market analysis, a competition analysis, targets and so on. This document will enable you to free yourself of emotions and assess what your prospects of success really are.

In other words, your business plan will be like a measuring stick that will test the feasibility of your plan and give you an objective view of the idea. This way, you'll be able to fine tune everything as necessary before you start up your business.

FUNDING

You'll certainly need money to start up your business, whatever it is. Of course, if you run an e-shop from home selling fabric nappies and clothes made of organic cotton, it will not be as demanding in terms of initial investment as opening a brick-and-mortar shop with the same assortment. However, if you do need – at least at the start – a financial injection from investors and creditors, these people will naturally want to know what exactly you intend to do and when they will get a return on their investment.

Investors should be able to learn everything important about your company, your idea and how you intend to implement it from your business plan. After reading it they should understand that:

- You've established your company after careful consideration.
- Your business intent is viable.
- The information – and money, if any – you have gathered so

far has been used for transforming the "mere" idea into a meaningful and constructive intent.

- You've done research – you are aware of the situation on the market and your competition's activities, so you have a good idea as to how your company will achieve success.
- You know your price and that your goods or services will be saleable.

If you need financial resources, you must be able to "sell" your idea. That means presenting it to potential investors in the best way possible. This is when your business plan may be of great help, especially if you lack experience in sales, presentations or convincing people. It doesn't matter how good your idea is, nobody will give you their trust or money if they feel that your thoughts are hazy and chaotic, and the same applies to your operation schedule and outlook for the future!

A BIRD'S-EYE PERSPECTIVE

When you start your business, you will tend to focus on everyday details. There are going to be days when you'll have to focus on maintaining the company for the next morning. Will the supplier deliver the flowers you need to decorate for a wedding with two hundred guests? Will your client pay your invoice in a timely manner so that you can pay the rent and freight fees?

Focusing on details is alright (unless you're getting lost in them over the long term). Nevertheless, running a business means building up a viable company that will be successful in the long term. So, you mustn't get swallowed up in details and secondary issues. You need to keep a detached, or bird's-eye, perspective.

A business plan is a useful instrument in this respect. Only when you see things from a wider, detached perspective can you assess the future of your company – and it will be easier for you to estimate the time required for certain achievements. If you're not ready to commit to your company for many years to come, then you're not ready to start doing business for yourself. If you don't feel enough determination or have faith in the longevity of your business, you'd better change tack and abandon your thoughts of starting a business. The power of the mind is immense and your doubts about your ability to succeed will materialize sooner or later.

YOU WILL BE READY FOR GROWTH

If you want to grow a flower, you need to provide the best conditions for its growth. You can learn what you need to know about growing flowers from a book. The same applies to business development. Your business plan is your guide to nurturing your company into a "flower". Of course, you can make adjustments at any time to correspond with reality and your expectations.

Imagine the following scenario: Your company is successfully growing and you – on the basis of a certain decision – are following the path you consider to be the right one. Let's say you've opened a foreign language textbook shop. The company is flourishing, and one day you get an interesting offer to start selling fiction as well. You would regret it if you didn't take the chance, and so you accept the offer. A quick look at your business plan would show you that you're diverting from the route you've planned. What might seem like a good decision today doesn't always pay off in the future. Diversifying your products may result in the loss of your hard-earned position in the language textbook market in the future.

Your business plan helps you stick to the pre-set course, and when you divert from it, it will help you find your way back. And one more thing... If you get used to doing business in accordance with the plan, the paper document will get into your blood and you will eventually follow your instincts when it comes to taking strategic decisions.

YOU WILL SAFEGUARD SUCCESS

Your business plan will increase the probability of your company's success, because you will be prepared for advertising costs and marketing investments. You will anticipate tax payments and possible losses, and you won't get derailed by fluctuations in customer numbers during different periods. You'll have anticipated any obstacles when writing your business plan, so you'll be ready for them, at least in theory. Anticipating possible problems and knowing how to avoid them is a sure way to remain one step ahead of your competition –leading you closer to success!

"I'm not the kind who opens up when meeting anybody. I'm fine if I can talk about my work or private life problems with my husband or best friend. After all, I was only able to start up my business thanks to my husband, who invested all the money he had inherited from a well-to-do relative so I was able to build a plant manufacturing parts for lorries. I know it is not exactly a woman's sphere, but I knew what I was going into as I had worked as a manager for a car manufacturer before. Two years ago I got into a position where I was forced to expand my manufacturing, which meant taking out a loan, this time from a bank. I had to give a presentation to strangers who, unlike my husband, had never heard of me or my work. I didn't regret the

time spent when writing up my business plan because I probably impressed the clerks and they eventually approved my loan."
(Donna, 43, UK)

WHAT NEEDS TO BE THERE

Now you know why it is so important to have a business plan. But what should be in it and how should you write it? Don't worry, even if you're a novice in business, you'll be able to do it easily if you know everything you need to.

In your business plan, you should describe your business targets, tools for achieving them, organizational structure, job positions, your competitive advantage, funding, return on investment (ROI) and the like. In principle, it will be a description of how your business should work.

Let's divide writing up the business plan into several steps that you can easily take one after another.

BASIC INFORMATION ABOUT YOUR COMPANY

The intent should first include basic information about your company and its organizational structure, your business concept.

A DESCRIPTION OF YOUR COMPANY

In this part you will describe your company more thoroughly, including details such as "I'll run my business from home, only online", and so on. You'll explain in what industry your company will operate, and describe the product or service you'll be selling. You should describe in the same detail your company structure, specifying the number of employees you intend to have and defining their duties.

MARKET RESEARCH

This part of your business plan will help you analyse the market and sum up facts that are necessary for achieving success. It is principally a description of the market environment. Especially for new entrepreneurs, it is very useful to describe the market's characteristics in great detail including the following aspects:

- **Potential customer/target market**

  Use the description you've written before. Describe thoroughly who your customer is.

- **Competition**

  Use the research you carried out when you were assessing whether there is space for your product or service on the market. Describe your competition.

This part concerning market analysis is particularly useful when giving presentations to potential investors and partners. The market changes constantly, which means you will need to continuously update the information along with it.

COMPETITIVE ADVANTAGE

Describe here the uniqueness of your product or service, or the original way in which you are going to offer it to your customers. You may mention the competitive advantage in your company slogan that your customers will see on your website, in promotional materials and so on. Just make sure you communicate it to your clients in order to benefit from it.

Do you still remember the remark that a product must satisfy the customer's need and desire? Now is the time to write down how and why this is the case for your product or service.

BUSINESS MODEL

This part answers the question of how your product or service is going to make money. More precisely, how you will get the money from your customer's pocket to yours. Write down the various sources you think your income will come from. Make it clear how you are going to sell to these sources and what distribution channels you'll choose. And remember to describe your pricing policy.

FINANCIAL PLANS

This part should include information about the current financial stability of your company and the outlook for the future. Describe the costs linked to your product. Specify here the results you expect in the following year and the next five to ten years after that. Put down the date by which you expect to see a return on your investment and when your business will become profitable.

MARKETING

Marketing is a substantial part of running a business and it doesn't matter if you're just starting your business up or if it is already established. Although marketing does require significant investment (not only in terms of money, but also time, ideas, surveys, etc.), I don't recommend skimping on it. Many potential investors will want to know what promotional ideas you have for both your product or service and the company, as they know very well that brand awareness is crucial for success. If you don't know what we're talking about, don't worry. In other chapters we will focus on marketing in more detail. For more tips about marketing and overall business visit my blog at **www.alexandrajohn.com**.

CHECKLIST

If you want to make sure you haven't omitted anything in your business plan, look at the following checklist of questions and add any missing information to the text. You can tick the questions off as you answer them.

- In which field do I want to run my business?
- What products or services do I offer?
- What is my competitive advantage?
- What are my company targets?
- What is my vision?
- Why will it pay off to invest in my company?
- What growth potential does my company have?
- Who is my potential customer?
- How many such customers are there in the market?
- Who are my competitors (competing for the same customer)?
- How do I set my prices? Will I be competitive?
- How will I promote my company?
- What manufacturing process do I use?
- What are my costs linked to manufacturing the goods or providing the services?
- Will I need employees?
- What will be their roles?
- Will I need consultants or expert cooperation?

- What problems could arise in the following one to five years?
- How will I cope with such complications?
- What profit do I expect?
- What are my start-up costs?
- How will I cover these costs?
- When will my company start generating profit?
- How long will I need loans for?
- What are my financial targets in the following one to five years?

Thoroughly elaborated answers to these questions will provide you with the necessary background material for compiling your business plan. You only need to arrange them logically. The truth is that starting up a business requires sufficient input of information, and if you haven't found the answers to any of these questions yet, then keep asking and searching.

 ## QUESTIONS TO CONSIDER 

DO I REALIZE THE IMPORTANCE OF MY BUSINESS PLAN?
It is always a good idea to have your business plan readily at hand.

HAVE I WRITTEN UP MY BUSINESS PLAN?
Allow enough time for writing it.

Chapter 6

Money comes after nothing else

How to get financing for your business

Financing your business will probably be the greatest challenge you will have to face in your new role. But before you start searching for possible resources, you should first fully understand how much money you will really need.

POSSIBLE EXPENDITURES

Naturally, the amount depends on the specific type of business, as well as its location – for example, whether you'll be doing business on the Internet or elsewhere. Whatever the case is, the expenditures you should anticipate include:

- Initial start-up fees (administrative fees, etc.)
- Cash desk/point of sale system, accounting software
- Rent for suitable premises (office, shop, place of business, etc.)
- Reconstruction or renovation
- Purchase of necessary equipment (for your office, shop, place of business, etc.)
- Product manufacturing
- Inventory
- Office supplies
- Telephone lines, Internet connection
- Utilities

- Service and maintenance (IT support, machine and device maintenance and repairs, etc.)
- Salaries for employees including national insurance
- Legal fees, permits and licences
- Taxes
- Websites
- Signwriting (signboard, orientation signs, door plates, etc.)
- Design of your company logo, business cards, promotional materials, etc.
- Advertising and marketing expenditures
- Professional development and compulsory employee training
- Don't forget insurance!

This list of items is only approximate, since setting up an e-shop selling toys requires different kinds of expenditures than opening a dance studio, for example. Some of the items might not be relevant to you, while your list may include some that are missing here.

Whatever the case, you should have a sufficient financial reserve at the start, as your company is unlikely to generate profit immediately. It may also take some time before you receive your first income or start earning amounts that will cover at least the major common operating expenses. Initial costs may also radically rise due to unexpected or unpredictable circumstances, so it is very important to take a pencil and paper and make an estimate of the anticipated sum before you start searching for a suitable investor. Investors will want to know exactly how much will have to be invested and specifically in what. Therefore, you should make an approximate "cash-flow" for the first six months of your business, taking into account all initial costs (i.e. what you'll need to invest before you actually start up your business) as well as regular monthly expenditures and expected income.

The detailed and clearly arranged list of expenditures should also include a reserve for necessary and unexpected expenditures.

WHERE ARE YOU GOING TO GET THE MONEY?

Once you have compiled your list, it is the right time to have a look at the various possibilities for financing your company.

LOANS

This option usually comes to mind first, although it is the most complicated one. Many new entrepreneurs apply for a business loan from a bank, but not many people succeed in getting one. Again, we need to bear in mind that a bank is an exacting investor who is primarily after profit. A bank's shareholders don't care about helping you with your certainly noble idea. I don't mean this ironically, I just don't want to entertain your false hopes. Money is their priority.

Banks obviously protect their shareholders' interests, so each entrepreneur needs to submit documents evidencing their reliability when applying for a loan. Banks are interested in your previous income tax returns, financial statements, budgets with expected cash flows and the history of the loans you've had so far. It is even harder for beginners who don't have any such documents. That's when you need your business plan. Go through it once again and focus on whether the bank may derive from it the following:

- **It is going to get its money back, while earning money by providing you the loan**

  The bank is not lending you the money because you have beautiful brown eyes or because you can sew original leather bags that people will enjoy carrying around. If they approve your application, they are doing so because it is good for their business, which is lending money for interest, and because you're probably giving them your property as collateral.

- **Thanks to the loan your business is going to grow faster**

  You should probably buy that lovely sofa for your waiting room with money from other sources. The bank wants to know how you will use the loan effectively, not how you will furnish your premises.

- **Your intentions are worth supporting**

  You need to catch their interest, so it is important to be able to explain clearly, briefly and also grippingly what your business is about. You don't need to describe everything in the greatest detail in one single document. Bank lending advisors are only human and reading through a wall of text will only exhaust them or put them off.

  At the same time, you shouldn't give monosyllabic replies – check that your business plan really describes the key aspects of your business and contains essential information about your intentions and how you're going to implement them.

- **You're able to implement your idea**

  It is not only about a promising idea. What also matters is who will be implementing it. Like it or not, you're also selling yourself to the bank, not just the business, so don't only talk about your plans, but also talk about yourself – of course, in connection with work, not about your experiences on your last holiday in Greece.

- **What you are going to give as collateral**
  A great business plan is fundamental, but it is not enough on its own. The bank requires guarantees that it is going to get its money back and will investigate what your (or your guarantors') assets are. Collateral typically takes the form of real estate. If the bank likes your business idea, it will carry out its own analysis of these assets.

It is quite possible that you'll eventually come to the conclusion that there's a different banking product that is more suitable for you. For instance, unsecured credit, which is not primarily intended for new entrepreneurs, doesn't require you put your property up as collateral and therefore doesn't have such strict criteria.

Remember that if you don't succeed at one bank, you may get a loan from another one. Banks differ in their criteria for lending money to small entrepreneurs. But before you actually call in to any bank, you should first find out what the current interest rates are (as these may be subject to change on a daily basis).

Don't be afraid to consult more institutions so that you can compare different offers.

It will take some time before you get a decision and even if the decision is positive and the loan is approved, don't expect to have the money in your account the next day. However, the day you receive the finance you will start repaying it according to the agreed schedule. Loans are usually repaid in monthly instalments over several years.

"The truth is that business may seem to be a non-binding game until you get a loan. You'll be leaving the bank feeling over the moon after they approve your loan, since it wasn't guaranteed that they would! But the joy is soon followed by fear as you start to worry if you can really repay it. At least in my case, I quickly became very nervous. I had many sleepless nights fretting that I wouldn't be able to amass the amount due each month. My parents and friends were telling me I was overdoing it and that I'd certainly make it, but I had terrible thoughts running through my head and I was picturing what would happen if I failed as an entrepreneur."
(Dominique, 29, Barbados)

INVESTORS

If you don't want to apply for a bank loan for some reason, another option is to find an investor, meaning somebody who is in the opposite situation as you: somebody without his or her own idea who has enough money and is willing to invest it in a business that is profitable or at least interesting, but certainly with great potential. Since investors are often real people rather than legal entities, you will have to be much more persuasive when giving your presentation to them than to the bank.

• Angel investors or business angels

The term "angel" doesn't mean that all you need to do is knock and the investor will open the door. Quite the contrary, it is not easy to catch an angel investor. However, if your company is unique, you may succeed.

Angel investors are usually people who've made money with their own successful business and now want to maximize it by investing in new and interesting things. They know a great deal about business and risks, which influences how they approach people interested in their finance, or applicants for want of a better word.

An angel is a person willing to invest in a start-up company in exchange for capital participation, usually in the form of priority shares or convertible bonds. Angels are considered to be one of the oldest resources of capital for new entrepreneurs; the term was originally used for wealthy patrons who funded theatre plays on Broadway at the beginning of the 20th century. (9)

Angel investors care about the following in particular:
- Whether or not the company/team has some relevant experience.
- If they understand the market they're about to enter.
- The products and technology.
- The competition and the company's advantages.

These aspects will also be important to them:
- The size of the share in your company that is being offered (angels are not usually looking to be major shareholders as they would rob you of your motivation).
- How and when they will get their money back.
- The expected ROI in the following three to five years.
- How much money you would like the "angel" to invest (angel investors usually put up sums ranging between £10,000 and £250,000; higher amounts are considered to be "venture capital").

Investors require sufficient protection of their investments (in partnership contracts or in company documents such as the articles of association), protection in following rounds of funding (pre-emptive rights, options, etc.) and the option to walk away from the company after a specified time period (typically after three to five years).

You can see an example of how angels work on the TV show **"Dragons' Den"**, where four successful entrepreneurs listen to new entrepreneurs pitching their business plans. Those whose projects and ideas are thought to be viable are offered a monetary investment in exchange for a share in their company.

If you have watched an episode of "Dragons' Den", you know that angels are very picky. They definitely prefer lucrative ideas, so if you get the chance to present your business intentions to a potential angel, you need to pull out all the stops and do the best you can. Make sure the presentation showcases your entrepreneurial spirit, your heart and your ideas. Unlike the bank, angels care about chemistry, whether there's a connection between the two of you and if you are on the same page. You should also realize that a business angel will bring more to your project than just money. These people have rich experience, know-how and contacts, an asset that, when shared with you, will prove extremely useful and for which you would otherwise have to pay a fortune. After all, the success of the business is also in their interest.

There are a number of organizations through which you can find business angels, such as the Angel Investment Network (www.angelinvestmentnetwork.co.uk) and the UK Business Angels Association (www.ukbusinessangelsassociation.org.uk). If you are in a non-English speaking country, don't be afraid to present your idea in English and your local language if you think it has potential – you can also consider presenting your project via the Internet or the possibility of gaining "start-up capital" from abroad through a "start-up" project such as MicroVentures (www.microventures.com/startups), gust (www.gust.com) or BAN (www.eban.org).

• Private equity/venture capital

Venture capitalists are people or companies (private capital funds) who, similar to angel investors, provide money either by increasing the registered capital or with a loan above the amount of the registered capital. These finances are typically provided to companies that have been doing business for some time and want to expand – in exchange for a share in the company and, hence, having the right of veto in some fundamental decisions (in the case of a private investor they become a shareholder of the company, if the investor is a fund then the shareholders are the administrators of the fund).

The intention of this partnership agreement will most likely be to transform the business into a joint-stock company, where the venture capitalist will become a shareholder. Therefore, you should make sure that you are ready to accept somebody else telling you what to do and perhaps even how. If you make a profit, the venture capitalist will profit too; if you fail, the investor loses money. When financers decide whether or not they will invest in your company, the main factor usually isn't the guarantee of a return on their investment, but rather the attractiveness and potential profitability of your business plan.

For further information, you should consult the appropriate industry body and public policy advocate for the private equity and venture capital industry. In the UK, for example, this is the British Private Equity & Venture Capital Association (BVCA) (www.bvca.co.uk).

• Sleeping partner

A sleeping partner is someone who invests money into your business but doesn't participate in the actual running or management of the company. However, this partner is entitled to look at company documents or into your accounts at any time.

In exchange for investing money into the company, this sleeping partner has a right to a share in the profit, but they also share any losses. That is, if the company is in the red, the sleeping partner's share decreases by a previously agreed percentage. When entering into a silent partnership, it is certainly a good idea to stipulate that your sleeping partner shall share to the same extent in both profit and loss.

If you acquire additional sleeping partners, you must enter into an agreement with each of them separately. Of course, you should definitely engage a good lawyer to write such agreements.

Take a look around, go through your address book and mobile phone. A sleeping partner can be a relative or friend of yours, or even a total stranger who finds your business plan interesting. It may be a partner company or your supplier.

And one more thing... It is possible that you might come across a suitable investor through a lucky encounter at a networking event. Many such groups and gatherings of entrepreneurs and investors are organized, for instance, by regional Chambers of Commerce, organizations such as the Federation of Small Businesses (FSB, www.fsb.org.uk) and the Angels Investment Network, discussed earlier – all with the aim of supporting entrepreneurship.

GOVERNMENT SUPPORT

If you are currently unemployed, you may be eligible for help from the government to set up your own business. A New Enterprise Allowance (NEA), for example, can provide money and support for your start-up if you're getting certain benefits. In order to be eligible, you must be aged eighteen or over, have a business idea and receive one of the following benefits:

- Jobseeker's Allowance (or your partner does)
- Employment and Support Allowance (or your partner does)
- Income Support, if you're a lone parent or you're sick or disabled

There are various types of government-backed support and finance available for businesses, including:

- Grants
- Finance and loans
- Business support, such as mentoring and consultancy
- Funding for small and medium-sized businesses and start-ups

Any money you get doesn't affect your housing benefit, tax credits, income taxes, universal credit or Access to Work grant.

Of course, the truth is that such help is not given to everyone who asks for it, so you must prepare your application thoroughly. A specialist will assess your business idea. If it has potential, you'll be signed up to the scheme and get a business mentor. You will only be able to claim financial support if your business plan is approved and you begin by working at your business for a minimum of sixteen hours a week. (For more information, see www.gov.uk/new-enterprise-allowance.)

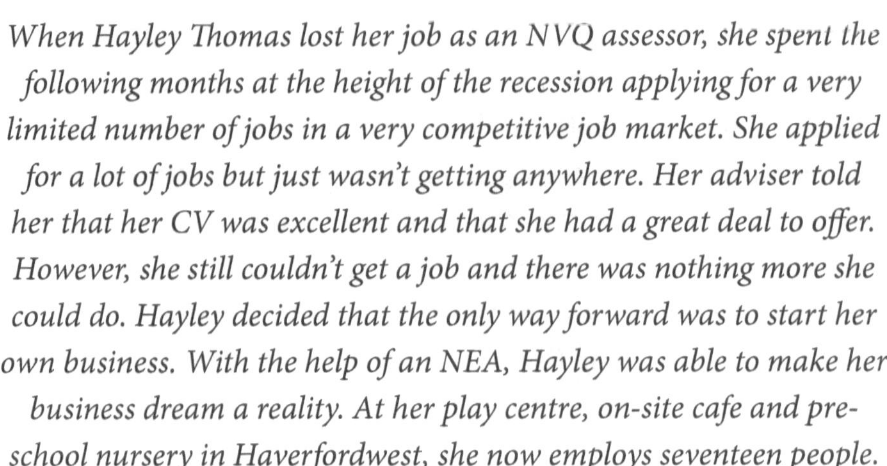

When Hayley Thomas lost her job as an NVQ assessor, she spent the following months at the height of the recession applying for a very limited number of jobs in a very competitive job market. She applied for a lot of jobs but just wasn't getting anywhere. Her adviser told her that her CV was excellent and that she had a great deal to offer. However, she still couldn't get a job and there was nothing more she could do. Hayley decided that the only way forward was to start her own business. With the help of an NEA, Hayley was able to make her business dream a reality. At her play centre, on-site cafe and pre-school nursery in Haverfordwest, she now employs seventeen people.

(Hayley Thomas, UK)

BUSINESS INCUBATORS

As the name suggests, a business incubator enables new entrepreneurs to gain their initial hands-on experience in a protected environment – to toughen them up before they jump into the ice cold waters of real life market conditions. They also provide access to a range of resources from business angel networks to high-speed Internet and low-rate central location space. There is understandably a lot of competition for space, so it is important to spend time researching which is the right one for you. Unfortunately, applying for a grant is usually a lengthy process with a lot of red tape and uncertain results.

In addition to subsidised offices and manufacturing premises, incubators usually offer support in the form of consultancy, which may concern marketing, accounting or taxes. In the UK, besides the big players such as My Incubator, Google Campus and TechHub, universities including Oxford, Loughborough and Lancaster also have a wide range of incubation initiatives. Business incubators strive to develop high growth potential businesses and help them to thrive, supporting entrepreneurship at the local and national level. They are usually not about money and financial loans, although you may get information about the grants currently available for new entrepreneurs.

FAMILY, FRIENDS, PARTNER

Even though this option may seem to be the easiest, it should be a last resort. The truth is you'll probably agree on a lower interest rate and a longer loan term, or even irregular instalments with your relatives, friends or life partner, because they know you better than the bank and they trust you. But, if your business doesn't fare very well, you may not feel comfortable when you are in everyday contact with your "creditors".

There is also a risk that the "debt" will eventually affect your relationship, even if everything goes smoothly. Can you imagine paying a New Year's visit to your aunt who keeps asking you when you will finally be able to pay back the rest of the money as she's unexpectedly decided to buy a new fitted kitchen?

You can prevent such complications by presenting your business plan to the person you ask for the money and by discussing everything thoroughly before you set the rules of the game. In this way, you can avoid the risk that the person will later meddle in your business, telling you what you should or shouldn't do. Don't forget to enter into a formal/certified agreement including details about the sum loaned, the interest rate and the maturity date. Clear agreements equal good friends and even relatives.

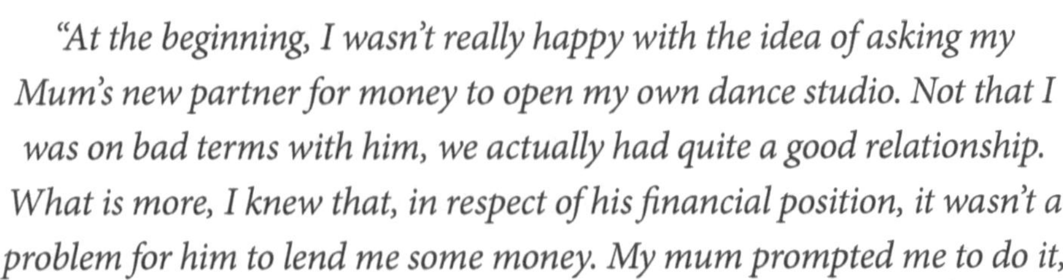

"At the beginning, I wasn't really happy with the idea of asking my Mum's new partner for money to open my own dance studio. Not that I was on bad terms with him, we actually had quite a good relationship. What is more, I knew that, in respect of his financial position, it wasn't a problem for him to lend me some money. My mum prompted me to do it, arguing that it would be better than having to pay off a debt to the bank. But I was afraid he might pressure me to increase my price for lessons over Christmas dinner, for example, so that I would be able to return the money sooner. Or perhaps he would disagree with my investment choices. And what would mum do if I had a disagreement with him? Finally, my grandma knocked some sense into me by telling me: 'Do you want your own dance studio? You do. Do you have your own money? No, you don't. Now you have the chance to get the sum you need, so grab it for Christ's sake and start doing something!' In the end, it turned out that my mum's partner had the same concerns, so we drew up a very detailed contract. This should ensure a good atmosphere over the Christmas dinner table this year."

(Marie, 25, Germany)

PERSONAL SAVINGS

A tempting solution to the problem of financing is to fund your business using your own savings, as it will keep you independent. But don't forget that in this case you're the only one who's bearing all the business risk.

Before you choose this option and use the funds from your life or pension insurance, or you sell your summer house (your only financial reserve for emergencies), you need to be absolutely certain that your company is viable. If you, God forbid, go bankrupt, you'll be left with nothing at all, with no means to repay your debts or unexpected expenditures – which you certainly don't want.

HOMEOWNER LOANS

Banks which specialize in mortgages typically offer mortgages strictly bound to investment in property, but also homeowner loans. This type of loan enables property owners to raise funds for any purpose, including business, by securing the loan against the borrower's existing property.

In comparison with an unsecured loan, the advantage of a homeowner loan is a lower interest rate (the bank undertakes minimal risk as they have your property as collateral), a longer term and the possibility to borrow a large amount. The negative of such a loan is, of course, the fact that you're securing it with your property, which you risk losing in the case of insolvency. If the collateral is the flat you live in, you would be in immense trouble. Moreover, as is the case for any other bank loan, you must document that you're able to repay it. Unlike business angels, venture capitalists and sleeping partners, if your venture is unprofitable, the bank will definitely **not** share in your loss.

CROWDFUNDING

Crowdfunding is a means of gathering money for implementing an idea by attracting a sufficient number of contributors from the general public. You can present your idea to those who might be interested in it via a crowdfunding website. Besides accumulating money for your start-up, this also enables you to start to build your reputation even before you "open your shop".

Crowdfunding is used in many countries around the world as a resource for financing artistic and non-profit activities (releasing a CD or publishing a book, holding cultural or other public events) as well as business ideas. The UK's largest crowdfunding platform is crowdfunder.co.uk; in the US, the most popular website of this kind is probably Kickstarter.com (although there are many others working on the same principle).

A great advantage of crowdfunding is the fact that, unlike with a loan or credit you can, to a greater extent, influence the outcome by your approach and activity. However, even crowdfunding has its fundamental "buts" that need to be considered:

- **You're not getting the money for free**
  In order for crowdfunding to work, you first need to generate a buzz around your cause – ideally with emotion and humour. And if the public response is positive, they will expect to receive the benefit you've offered. You can motivate people with anything – from offering your product for free to discounts or having your benefactor's name on the front wall of your shop; again, what matters is your original and creative approach.

- **Not all applicants succeed**
  Your idea must be original, viable and presented in an attractive way so that it wows the "crowd". Realistically, crowdfunding is unlikely to be sufficient as your only source of funding, but never say never – your drive and zeal for the cause can work wonders!

Did you know there were so many possibilities for funding your business? True, all of them have their pitfalls, but you'll certainly pick the one that will best suit your personal situation and your specific business intentions. And if one option fails, try another one. Be flexible and don't get easily put off.

 QUESTIONS TO CONSIDER 

IS MY LIST OF EXPENDITURES READY?

Even a rough estimate is enough to start gathering the relevant information that is important for getting the money you need.

HAVE I FOUND A PERSON WILLING TO INVEST IN MY BUSINESS?

If not, think about what your possibilities are and who your potential investor may be.

DO I HAVE TO TAKE OUT A LOAN?

If you do, find out what type of loan is the most suitable for you.

HOW MUCH MONEY DO I HAVE IN MY PERSONAL ACCOUNTS?

If your savings are substantial enough that they can be used to start up your business and you'll still be left with a sufficient sum for "rainy days", then that is an ideal solution. You can avoid taking out a loan and paying interest. But it would be risky and short-sighted if you were to invest all the money you have in the world.

Chapter 7

Choose your destination, but expect your route to change

Describe your company processes and match them with your personal schedule

In your business plan you've described your daily routine, and now it's time to define how you'll actually implement it. Start outlining your company's fundamental processes. What matters most? A business process model is a sequence of activities performed in a specific and constant order with the purpose of achieving better business results. Each company process has a clearly defined beginning and end, and it keeps repeating in cycles so that you can manage, evaluate and change it at any point in the process. This means you'll be able to better organize your work, react more flexibly to customer impulses and so on. These are obvious reasons why it is beneficial to give attention to your processes.

Even if your company is (at least at the beginning) a rather small one, the extent of all the activities, and thus company processes, may be bigger than you expected and include things such as:

- Manufacturing
- Purchasing
- Sales
- Pricing
- Inventories and supplies
- Maintenance and cleaning

- Orders and invoicing
- Goods transport
- Company/product promotion

Virtually everything that happens in a company takes the form of a company process – organizing supplies, product development and handling customer orders. If you run, say, an e-shop, the model for the handling process may be as follows:

> Event: A customer orders and pays for goods online

> Activity: The e-shop receives an order

> Activity: Employee A locates, takes from the warehouse and packages the goods

> Activity: Employee B prints out a receipt and checks the order

> Activity: Employee B dispatches the package

> Event: The customer receives the goods

The business process either creates value itself (its output being a manufactured product, provision of a service, etc.) or it supports another key process which does create value. A simple example is the handling of a complaint regarding defective goods:

1. Customer's request for replacement goods received.
2. Complaint analysis.
3. Decision taken by the employee responsible as to whether to accept or refuse the complaint.
4. Now, since there are two possible ways to further proceed, it is better to draw the specific course of events on paper as a simple "development graph".
5. Communication with the client.
6. If the complaint is accepted, it is necessary to deliver a new product to the customer.
7. Termination of the complaint procedure.

When proposing company process models, there are many templates available on the Internet for you to use (e.g. www.process.st; www.laserfiche.com; www.auraportal.com). Another useful tool is the Visio application from Microsoft that allows you to visualise and create processes in Excel and document them.

RUN TESTS

Early versions of work processes often look perfect on a graph, a piece of paper or a computer screen, but there are no guarantees that they will work well in practice. That's why it is pragmatic to try out the proposed processes before applying them. This way you can avoid potentially serious trouble. Always ask yourself "What if" and "What's the next step?" You should go through the complete business process and test it without customer participation. Even if you later come across complications, write down what needs to be changed.

At the very beginning, whether you are self-employed or have ten employees, you must be 100 per cent sure that everybody in the company knows exactly how the business and other processes should work.

"I own an agency specializing in holding conferences and various company and social events. At first I made fun of business process modelling – do you really expect me to make a graph before I come to work specifying that when I arrive at work I should open the doors, walk through them and shut them behind me? My husband, who's been doing business for many years, told me: 'Don't laugh. You'll see. You'll appreciate it when you have to hand over a description of what is happening in your company.' In the end, his words proved right. I found out that an employee I had entrusted with organizing an important event had 700 invitations printed and sent without having definitely confirmed the venue. She said the hotel had promised her that she could have the date – unfortunately, only on the phone. I realized that even though I may know what the sequence of steps to be taken is, my colleagues may have different ideas."

(Sabine, 30, Sweden)

A GOOD PLAN MINIMIZES LOSSES

While making company processes, you should simultaneously take into account your personal time schedule (let's call these "personal processes") and figure out how you can combine the two. Running your own business requires a great amount of time, and if you are busy in your private life, you won't cope without good planning. You may have to give up some social activities, but a good plan can minimize such "casualties".

If you have problems planning your time, read some books on time management. There are plenty of them on the market. Out of the many available, I'll mention two: Dan S. Kennedy's, *No B.S. Time Management for Entrepreneurs* (Entrepreneur Press, 2013) and Kevin Kruse's, *15 Secrets Successful People Know About Time Management* (The Kruse Group, 2015).

Doing business on the Internet gives you the option to make plans more flexibly, because even if the total amount of work that needs to be done doesn't change, you can work when it suits you. This is an ideal situation for a mother of small children. The downside of this is an irregular daily schedule and the frequent necessity to work regardless of the time of the day, even at night.

OPENING HOURS

If you run a brick-and-mortar shop, or any other business with opening hours (a restaurant, massage studio, language school, centre for mothers with children, etc.), you have to be available at least during the hours you're open. In time, you'll certainly have employees, but at the beginning it is necessary that you are present, which you will also need to take into account when planning your working hours.

On the other hand, it is not wise to limit yourself to just following your personal time preferences. You need to be there for your customers when it most suits them. It might be convenient to plan your calligraphy course for 10 am. However, if you'd like to attract anyone other than mothers on maternity leave, unemployed or retired people, it would be a better idea to schedule your workshop in the evening or at the weekend.

There's also no point in opening a bakery when you know you cannot function properly in the morning. In many cases, you should expect that you'll often need to work at the weekends – only very few shop owners and caterers can afford to be closed to prospective buyers for the whole weekend. And if you run a hotel or B&B, you can forget about weekends altogether – you'll need to work virtually non-stop.

The opening hours you choose will influence your work processes. If you have a sign on your door saying that you're open at 9 am, you'll need to be there an hour earlier to get everything ready in time. The same applies to the closing time – you need to allow time for counting your day's takings and cleaning. Therefore, your work process for the end of the day should be something like this:

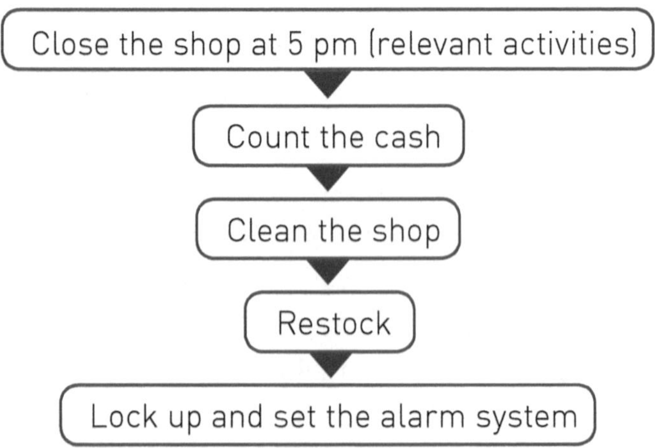

This description is, of course, only an illustration. You'll need to plan the process in much more detail.

THE ONLY GUARANTEE IS CHANGE

Flexibility is essential for entrepreneurs. Even if you are aware of the importance of planning and you are trying to outline the future as precisely as possible, don't expect to get everything right. Sooner or later you'll find that some planned processes simply don't work in practice. You shouldn't be surprised by that. Insisting rigidly on your original expectations leads nowhere. You should show some willingness to change things instead and react to current needs. After all, an important role of a business owner is to keep searching for new ways to make your company operate more efficiently.

Let's say you have a team of young people who dispatch products that are ordered online. One of the employees is responsible for packaging and shipping the goods, but there are so many orders now that this employee cannot do everything in a timely fashion. You're left with no other choice but to change the process. You'll transfer some of the duties to another employee and hire someone new to take over the remaining workload.

Your company will be growing, changing and developing, just the same as you. The way to entrepreneurial hell is paved with company owners who were obstinately convinced that "if it ain't broke, don't fix it." But consumers always expect something new and better, no matter how good or functional the original. Why do you think that TV advertisements present innovations such as yoghurt with "bigger pieces of fruit" or new toilet fresheners that are "now more practical in angular casing"? It only proves that the consumer desire for innovation is infinite. As a successful entrepreneur, you will simply have to get used to it and keep changing, otherwise you will have no chance of success.

After 15 years of working for an investment bank, Paula Fry decided to use her savings to follow her passion and start up a vintage and pre-loved fashion boutique.

"I loved the idea of recycling and reusing, plus vintage was just becoming main stream and we were teetering on the edge of a recession. Women were spending less on fast fashion and would rather buy quality than quantity."

She prepared well, doing research on the clients she had in mind, preparing her plan and completing a couple of business courses. The shop was opened in December 2009, just six months after she'd left the city.

Paula worked relentlessly: did social media, marketed herself and the boutique and was fortunate to land a monthly fashion column in Kent Life, along with lots of mentions in popular fashion magazines and daily newspapers. "But it just wasn't enough. I opened my online business to complement the shop and broaden the demographics for my sales, but I soon realised that having a retail shop AND an online presence was harder than I had ever imagined. I paid my bills and my staff, but there was never really anything for me after all those costs."

Reluctantly, after a couple of years, Paula had to go back into banking. But she kept her business going, working every spare hour to keep things afloat. However, this became a battle that was impossible to win. Then one evening she was suddenly inspired when she came across an online dress agency selling pre-loved designer items.

It was apparent that thousands of independent fashion shops all over the UK were struggling to be found.

"The following day, the principle idea for Fashionseeker was born, although I sat on it for nearly six months before I put the wheels in motion to get it going." (11)

(Paula Fry, UK)

QUESTIONS TO CONSIDER

ARE ALL OF MY COMPANY PROCESSES DRAFTED?

Go through all the activities related to your company operations and describe every step of each process.

HAVE I TESTED THEM?

Testing is how you can eliminate any discrepancies before the actual start of your business.

HAVE I WRITTEN DOWN MY PERSONAL SCHEDULE?

You must know this so that you can link it with your business plan.

Chapter 8

The captain is searching for her crew

Your employees may bolster your business or drag it under water, so you should pay attention when hiring

You're standing at the crossroads or slowly approaching it. At the moment, you may be quite positive about things. You don't need any employees as you're planning to open a small deli. But what about a year or two down the line? Are you sure that you can take care of a fast-growing company? Whether it is imminent or light years away, you should think about this issue.

First you need to find out whether hiring an employee will pay off, meaning does your profit exceed employment costs. If it does, to what extent are you able to use such an employee: full-time or part-time? Or will you be fine with occasional help from a temporary worker?

DO YOU REALLY NEED ANOTHER HELPING HAND?

Does it pay off for you to be a "girl Friday", or would it be more effective for you to find a helper (or more of them)? Try to honestly answer the following questions:

- Are you so busy with everyday operational activities that you cannot focus on marketing and advertising? Do you think that if this changed and you could fully dedicate yourself to sales support, your company would become more successful? Could it be that you're not utilizing yourself fully?

- If you hired somebody, would you be able to serve more clients? The fact that you can only do a certain amount of work may be limiting your business; by hiring a new employee or employees you could create space for expansion.
- Would hiring a new employee mean an improvement in the goods or services you offer to your customers? If you feel there is room to develop your services, you should immediately get to work. Hiring more workers is actually the least you can do.

Evaluate the actual contribution of any new employee and calculate carefully how much your profit would rise.

 DON'T BE TAKEN IN

Small company owners must hold a lot of posts in their business. Hence, they find the possibility of curtailing their workload by hiring a new employee very tempting. You presume that if you have someone who helps you, you'll have more free time, don't you? Maybe it's true. But don't forget that you will also need to invest quite a lot of time, especially when hiring the new employee, in the recruitment process, subsequent training of the employee and all other obligations each employer must meet.
So do you really need a new workforce or could you manage by reorganizing your time? It might pay off to attend a time management seminar where you can discover the root causes of your excessive workload and find a solution. (12)

Be frank. Are you secretly hoping to find a soul mate in your employee and support in uncertain times? An employee is not your friend, regardless of how you feel about them. As an employee, this friend is primarily your inferior, and it would be a mistake to delegate your responsibility to him or her. The responsibility still lies on your shoulders, whoever you employ. It will probably be hard to be a friend and boss at the same time. Any attempts to mix private life with work mean you're walking on very thin ice, and in the long run you may jeopardize the company as well as your friendship. You should decide what is more important to you. And, if you want to employ your friends, it is in the best interest of everyone involved to clarify the rules of the game in advance.

Or it might be the other way around. You could make meaningful use of a new employee, but you are convincing yourself you'll manage it all on your own. But how long can you bear such a burden? And what will be the price you'll eventually pay? Do you realize that the price you'll pay for such false heroism could be your health or the break-up of your marriage and family?

Figure out why you're actually refusing to hire any help. Does it happen to be because you suffer from a feeling of being irreplaceable and you think that nobody else will do your job as well as you do? Such an attitude usually hides the fear of losing control, which in turn suggests low confidence. The remedy is to acknowledge and accept your value (and thus the value of others), to start trusting your colleagues and delegating tasks to them.

"Although I didn't want to admit it, I suffered from the 'great mother syndrome'. At least that's what I now call my former approach to my employees. I ran a restaurant with my husband. I took care of the cuisine and sup-

plies, and he served guests and was in charge of accounting. We employed a chef and a waiter and sometimes we had temporary workers. In fact, we didn't hire the chef until my husband couldn't take it any longer when I winced with pain every move I made. But I believed that if I didn't cook the menu myself, our guests wouldn't come back. And I had the same mistrust towards the waitress. The inevitable happened. By thinking that I was the only one who could do everything properly, I raised our employees and even my husband to be 'irresponsible kids' who were either 'naughty' or 'loafed about' as soon as I was out of sight. It was only when I ended up in hospital with back problems and on a drip that I realized where I was making the mistake."

(Florence, 44, France)

CALCULATE EVERYTHING CAREFULLY

So you've come to the conclusion that you can't do without another employee. Use a calculator to calculate to what extent you can afford new labour. Take into account the following expenditures.

RECRUITMENT PROCESS

While those searching for a job can do so via job websites for free, entrepreneurs need to pay for advertising. The service of recruitment agencies is also rather expensive.

TRAINING

Training your new employee to be perfectly capable of coping with his or her tasks will cost you, in addition to money, a lot of time.

WAGES

You won't get a lot of bang for your buck – this is also true for wages. You cannot expect long-term initiative, dazzling work tempo or loyalty to your company from an underpaid employee, even though at the beginning such an employee may be delighted to have the job. Money is money, although there are other important sources of motivation such as self-actualization, zest for work and so on.

BENEFITS

Don't forget to consider possible benefits for your employees such as coffee and tea or meal vouchers, for example.

INSURANCE AND TAXES

You must also include other costs such as taxes and national insurance payments. These make up a significant part of an employee's salary.

OVERHEADS

Costs for each job position, office rent and utilities (heating, electricity), sometimes even travel costs, clothing allowances, software licences, invoices for staff telephones or fuel and so on.

You can simply put the relevant amounts in this simple chart:

A	Your current profit	
B	Expected increase in profit after hiring a new employee	
C	Total of A + B = total increased income	
D	Expected salary	
E	Expected tax and insurance costs	
F	Other expected costs	
G	Total of D + E + F	
H	**Deduct G from C (i.e.: C – G)**	

If you get a negative number, hiring a new employee wouldn't pay off and you would have to subsidize the operation costs for this job position. If you get a positive number, it is fine. The ideal case is if the number in line C is higher than the sum in line G. If that is not so, the employee will probably cost you more than he or she is able to generate for the company. By deducting G from C you'll find out how hiring new workforce members will be reflected in your profit.

Now do you know what your decision is going to be? If you've come to the conclusion that in order to improve your company's prosperity you need a new employee, make sure you are clear on who exactly you're searching for.

WHAT MUST EACH ADVERTISEMENT INCLUDE?

Consider what exactly you expect from your new employee: what he or she should be capable of; what his or her education, skills and experience should be. Are you searching for somebody with extensive experience who won't require any training, or rather a fresh graduate who'll require some time to learn the ropes, but who will be flexible timewise and will be willing to work for a lower salary?

You need to be very specific in your advertisement. Only then can you expect reasonable responses. You should definitely include the following:

- **Company name and possibly a short presentation**
- **Job title**

  Avoid using inaccurate or confusing job titles, otherwise suitable candidates may ignore your advertisement. The same applies to writing a job title that sounds inappropriately sophisticated. If you're not actually searching for an employee for an international company, it is really useless to write "shop sales representative" when you need a shop assistant (even if it is for a shop selling luxury apparel).

- **Job description**
- **Full or part-time?**
- **Applicant requirements**

  The labour market is flexible these days and the same should apply to you (it is in your best interests). Besides full-time jobs there are other arrangements that might be more appropriate for your company needs, which we will look at further.

- **State appealing benefits and bonuses**

  If you don't know what to write, leave it out (presenting the use of the company microwave as a bonus would sound like making virtue out of necessity). Fresh graduates and people with vision may see working for "a young company with interesting products enabling employees to implement their own ideas" as a benefit.

- **Name and contact details of the person applicants should write to**

It is also sensible to include an application deadline and the region or exact place of work as well as the date of commencement. The big question is whether or not to publish the salary you are offering. If you want to avoid publishing this for strategic or other reasons, I recommend leaving this information for the personal interview stage or merely stating the possible salary range.

 ## FLEXIBLE WORKING 

Flexible jobs are frequently discussed, but employers are still afraid of them (fear of the "unknown", unfamiliarity with the relevant laws, fear of complicated organization, etc.). This often leads companies to deprive themselves of qualified and experienced employees, because for many applicants alternative forms of employment are the only option. Many consider flexibility as being one of the most important requirements when looking for work.

It is important to emphasize the following: alternative employment is not charity. It is actually a way of gaining a loyal and often highly qualified and experienced worker! I very much doubt you will regret it if you step off of the beaten track and hire a person meeting all your requirements who is – for one reason or another – not able to sit in the office from nine to five, Monday to Friday.

Of course, you first need to get straight what the employee's obligations will be and set the rules of the game (mutual trust will not come overnight and it is only natural that at the beginning there will be more lead and control on your part). If a mother of two-year-old twins tells you in an interview that if her children are ill she doesn't have anyone to look after them, you have the right to not want to tolerate her probable frequent absences as these would harm your business.

And what forms of flexible employment are there?

PART-TIME EMPLOYMENT

Shorter working hours mean lower salary, otherwise the employment conditions are the same as for full-time employees. Employees are still entitled to benefits as well as paid holiday.

JOB SHARING

This is when two employees share one job. For instance, a company hires two part-time assistants who split the role between them. This could mean that each works three days in row or any other arrangement that is agreed on between them and you. To make it work, these assistants must be a team that pulls together and informs each other in detail about work issues.

FLEXIBLE WORKING HOURS

An employee chooses the start and/or end of their working hours, or even the days, within the range allowed by the employer. In other words, you may determine that all the employees must be in the office from 9 am to 1 pm every day. Where they work from for the remaining hours is up to them.

VARIABLE HOURS

A variable hours contract enables the employer to assign work as and when needed, for instance, in accordance with the actual volume of orders or a particular "rush" of work. Particularly for industries that experience peaks and troughs, when there's a lot of work, the employer may require employees to work from Monday to Sunday, and the days off due at the weekend are taken on different days. Working time accounts are used, for instance, by construction companies, beauty salons and some shops. However, it does require a lot of admin.

COMPRESSED WORKING WEEK

A normal working week is squeezed into four days. Employees thus have three days off.

WORKING FROM HOME

Today this is quite common. It is up to you, the employer, how many hours you let your employees work from home. Naturally, it depends on the nature of their job, since it is not suitable for all jobs. This type of employment doesn't work when there is no strong mutual trust between the employer and employees or without very exact specified conditions. The employee's performance is supervised according to the amount of work done. This type of employment saves costs, for instance, a number of employees may share just one "hot desk" in the office.

WHERE TO SEARCH FOR THE RIGHT ONE

You know precisely who you're searching for, for what position and what you can offer them. All you need to do now is one final thing, probably the hardest one – to find such a person. Where and how can you hunt for the right people?

RECOMMENDATION FROM A TRUSTWORTHY PERSON

If you mention that you're searching for a new employee when chatting with friends or peers, you might immediately get a recommendation for somebody capable and trustworthy whose qualifications and experience are perfectly in line with your requirements. If you find, when you meet that person face to face, that you are birds of a feather, you can congratulate yourself. Finding an employee "on recommendation" from someone you trust is the ideal way.

RECOMMENDATION FROM ANOTHER EMPLOYEE

Sometimes your current employees may know of a suitable candidate for a new opening in your company. If you motivate them to recommend potential colleagues by offering them, for example, an appropriate bonus payable if the new recruit continues to work for the company after the probation period, once again you have a match made in heaven.

RELATIVES, FRIENDS AND ACQUAINTANCES

Giving a job to a relative or friend may be tempting, but you must tread very carefully so that your decision doesn't jeopardize your relationship or weaken your company. An undeniable positive of this option is the fact that you know the person very well. You know what he or she is capable of and what that person is like. Nevertheless, you should remember that if you hire somebody who is personally close to you, you need to approach him or her just as you would any other employee.

Most importantly, you shouldn't make compromises when it comes to qualifications and experience – you cannot afford to take on board your new and thus rather unstable ship somebody who could drag you down (and in the end, even themselves), despite his or her best efforts. Don't offer a job just because your sister "needs to get out and be in touch with other people" or "your poor uncle hasn't been able to find a job for the past three years". Imagine the atmosphere in a team (your company will certainly grow by hiring other people in the future) that includes somebody who doesn't have what it takes to do the job, but is unshakeable because they are your cousin.

Consider whether you would be able to cope with possible critical moments such as dealing with an argument between two employees, one of whom is your uncle; an increase in some employees' salaries, but not that of your relative; and so on. Problems may occur when you have to consider making redundancies. It is much harder to lay off somebody you have a personal bond with. What is more, you may easily fall prey to manipulation or even blackmailing from your relatives.

ADVERTISING ON JOB WEBSITES

Job websites can be used in two ways. They give you access to a database of CVs uploaded by potential applicants where you can search for suitable candidates. You may also place your job advertisement on the site, and job applicants can contact you by email or phone. Of course, it is more effective to choose job websites with a large number of viewers, although they will charge you for their service, rather than advertising for free on sites with lower traffic.

Be inventive when advertising your job opening. Put the offer on your company website and also use social networks. This will significantly extend your reach, and you'll be noticed by more potential candidates.

SOCIAL NETWORKS

LinkedIn serves the purpose of connecting professionals from different fields who discuss professional interests. LinkedIn was designed as a tool for collecting new contacts, so-called networking, but it will also help you find a suitable candidate for an opening in your company. You can search by entering various keywords (e.g. sales manager) and people who are interested in a new job often have a "looking for a new job" status, for example.

RECRUITMENT AGENCIES

In theory, a recruitment agency should find you a suitable applicant for any job. As these companies usually prefer to focus on specific areas (with big commissions), it pays to use their services in cases where you're looking for employees to fill key or specialist positions. You'll have less work to do, as these agencies will do the first round of selection (sieve) for you and you'll only interview serious candidates with relevant profiles and remuneration expectations.

JOB CENTRES

If you're searching for employees for less qualified jobs, you can turn to the job centre. The advantage of offering your vacancies at the job centre is that it doesn't cost much and it is also possible to get an allowance or subsidy. In the UK, for example, Jobcentre Plus offers recruitment advice and support to businesses including:

- Advisers who understand your recruitment needs and the local labour market.
- Help with the design and wording of your job vacancy advertisement.

- Assistance developing specific pre-employment training for new employees where needed.
- Suggestions for new recruitment methods for your company and ways to avoid exclusion, e.g. by offering flexible working.
- Opportunities for your existing employees to mentor people who want to work.
- An aftercare service once the recruitment process is over.

(www.gov.uk/jobcentre-plus-help-for-recruiters/recruit-ment-advice-and-support)

The various Jobcentre Plus employment schemes can help you recruit suitable employees as well as create opportunities for people looking for work.

The main disadvantages of using a job centre are that it is a rather time consuming (paperwork) and demanding process of employee selection. The "candidates" are also sometimes people who are interested in getting paid, but not in actually working and often include people who are hard to place on the labour market.

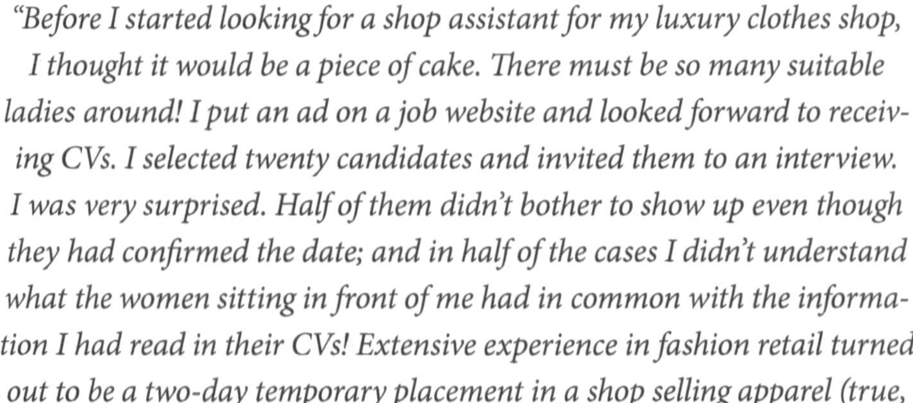

"Before I started looking for a shop assistant for my luxury clothes shop, I thought it would be a piece of cake. There must be so many suitable ladies around! I put an ad on a job website and looked forward to receiving CVs. I selected twenty candidates and invited them to an interview. I was very surprised. Half of them didn't bother to show up even though they had confirmed the date; and in half of the cases I didn't understand what the women sitting in front of me had in common with the information I had read in their CVs! Extensive experience in fashion retail turned out to be a two-day temporary placement in a shop selling apparel (true,

they also sold wellingtons and dungarees). Experience with sales seemed to mean rearranging the shelves in their uncle's second-hand bookshop. I was left with the last two CVs and – finally – the last applicant and I clicked. I now realize that having a loyal and hardworking employee is certainly not a matter of fact!"

(Abbie, 34, UK)

DON'T UNDERESTIMATE PREPARATION FOR INTERVIEWS

When you're sitting face to face with a stranger, who is perhaps even older or more experienced in professional matters than you, it can be hard to get a true feeling about that person. It can be nerve racking, yet you have to decide in a limited amount of time if they are the individual you're really looking for. I agree that personal interviews are not an easy discipline and it is a difficult situation for both parties.

Fortunately, just as the applicant prepares for the interview, so can you – well, actually, you should.

First of all, don't underestimate selecting the right place. Preferably, you should have the job interview in a meeting room on your company premises. This should be a representative space where you won't be disturbed and the applicant can get a feel for the company spirit. A meeting room is also impersonal enough that it doesn't distract anyone's attention. If you like, you can meet up in a quiet café, but in that case, you should explain to the candidate why the interview is not taking place on company premises.

Gather all the background materials on the applicant, including the printed CV, so that you can take down any notes (an open notebook may be seen as a barrier between the two of you, and typing may evoke the feeling that you're not listening). Take into account that 40 per cent of data in CVs are exaggerated or fabricated. Therefore, don't hesitate to check the references. Ask the references provided how they would describe what it was like to work with the candidate.

WHAT YOU SHOULD ASK, AND WHAT YOU SHOULDN'T

A job interview is not a duel or an exam. It is a joint effort to come to a conclusion as to whether you're the right employer for the candidate and the candidate is the right employee for you. Don't be aloof or too familiar. Create a friendly atmosphere in which you will feel relaxed (welcoming candidates with a smile and hand shake, offer them some coffee, tea or water, start with small talk by asking general questions about the journey, the weather and the like). However, bear in mind that a job interview is not just a chat over a cup of coffee – it should be a serious process with a clear outcome. You're the one who's in charge, so you invite the applicant to talk, ask about specific things, rather than merely having a casual conversation.

Ask the questions you've prepared beforehand. They may include some of the following:

1. What are the reasons you left/are leaving your previous job? Why are you looking for a new one?
2. Why did you decide to apply for this job and why in my company?
3. Why should I select you? What makes you better than/different from the others?
4. What are your strengths and weaknesses?

5. What have you achieved in your career so far? What is your greatest achievement?
6. Describe a person you consider to be your professional idol. Why do you admire this person?
7. What don't you like doing at work?
8. Describe a situation or process that you would've simplified or made more efficient in your previous/current job. How would you tackle this specific case in "our company"?
9. How do you settle disputes? Think of a specific past instance and describe what you did.
10. What are your expectations concerning salary?
11. If I choose you, and offer you the specified salary, what would another company have to do to poach you from us?
12. Where do you see yourself in two years' time? And in five years' time?
13. Do you have any questions for me?

Of course, you may ask more unusual questions aimed at finding out what the applicant thinks about him or herself, such as, "If my company were a motorway, what car would you be?" Or you could ask the applicant to describe a company-specific situation model.

If you are interviewing employees for a role that involves regular contact with customers or suppliers, try to prepare a short role play situation. For example, you (or a colleague/friend) play a customer or supplier with a complaint, and the candidate must settle the said complaint.

Should you need to assess the theoretical knowledge required for the given job (expert, legal), ask the applicants to take a short test.

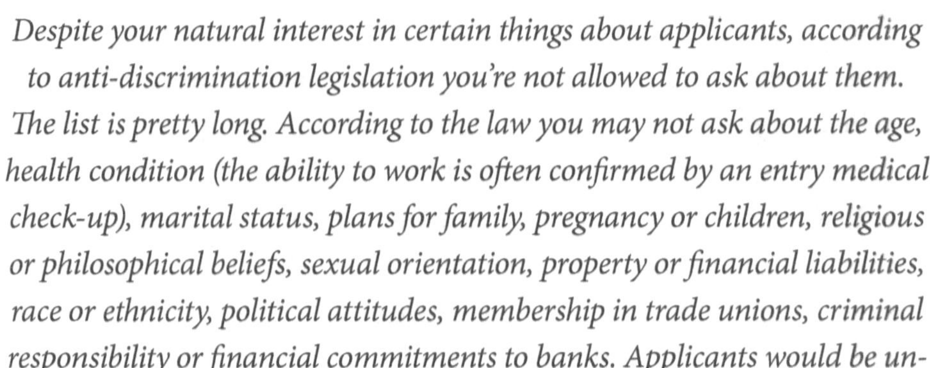

Despite your natural interest in certain things about applicants, according to anti-discrimination legislation you're not allowed to ask about them. The list is pretty long. According to the law you may not ask about the age, health condition (the ability to work is often confirmed by an entry medical check-up), marital status, plans for family, pregnancy or children, religious or philosophical beliefs, sexual orientation, property or financial liabilities, race or ethnicity, political attitudes, membership in trade unions, criminal responsibility or financial commitments to banks. Applicants would be unlikely to press charges against you, but a potential employer certainly suffers in the eyes of applicants if such questions are asked. (13)

You shouldn't be content with just what the applicants tell you, try to find out more about them. You have references so don't hesitate to verify them.

WHY TAKE TIME OVER YOUR SELECTION?

The final aspect of selecting the most suitable employee is really a mystery. You should take into account not only the qualifications and experience of the candidates, but also their character traits and fit with the company. You may also use your intuition, just be aware that first impressions are not always right and a person who seems confident and charming at an interview, may prove to be neither confident nor charming. On the other hand, someone who seems to be morose at first may prove to be a pleasant person in everyday contact. Their initial "grumpiness" may just be due to the stress of the job interview, which is not necessarily an indication of incapacity, but often an expression of interest in the opening.

If you're still not sure, and a sufficient number of candidates have applied, hold a second round of interviews. Don't put too much pressure on yourself and take your time before making a decision. Employing the wrong person will lead to complications and waste time and money – for example:

- Lengthy dismissal processes or making redundancy payments.
- Wages for overtime worked by employees who have to take over the job duties of the sacked person.
- Costs of the recruitment and training of a new employee.
- Reduction in productivity during the gap between employees.
- Decrease in the number of customers, if the dismissal of the employee affects customer services.

There is no denying it, people dislike overtime and don't want to do more than they have to. So, when one employee leaves, the working morale in the entire company may be affected. This can lead to mistakes, loss of goods and a decrease in the quality of customer service. I don't mean that you should reproach yourself for making a mistake when hiring a new employee – anyone can make a mistake. I just want to stress how important it is to dedicate enough time, attention and energy to the recruitment process, as its consequences will come back to haunt you in weal and woe. Not to mention that high employee turnover is never good for any company or its reputation.

QUESTIONS TO CONSIDER

DO I NEED EMPLOYEES?

Just because you cannot do everything right away doesn't mean you really need employees – sometimes things can wait.

CAN I AFFORD TO EMPLOY SOMEBODY ELSE?

Consider whether you actually have the money to hire someone, particularly in relation to what this person will contribute.

HOW MANY PEOPLE WILL I HIRE?

Think about what your new employees need to do, and decide whether you need to hire just one or a number of them.

AM I READY TO GIVE A JOB INTERVIEW?

Many books have been written on how to conduct job interviews correctly and choose the best candidate. In addition to the information in this chapter you may find inspiration from books such as Sean McManus and John Townsend's *Interviewer's Pocketbook* (Management Pocketbooks, 2014) which includes a lot of practical tips and techniques that you can make use of during job interviews.

Chapter 9

Lawyers and accountants – choose them wisely!

How to handle fiendish laws, cope with numbers and satisfy the tax office

Now we will look at two areas that usually trouble entrepreneurs, although they could easily cope with them if they tried a little harder: The legal aspects of business and taxes and accounting.

In order to start up your business successfully, you first need to handle a lot of questions concerning the law. Unless you have relevant education, the best solution is to hire a good lawyer who will help you not only with set up, but also with guidance in the future. Quality advice at the right time will spare you many problems that you would otherwise get bogged down with due to ignorance.

Let's begin with what needs to be done when you're starting your business. Then we'll move on to legal issues that you may come across later on.

SOLE TRADER OR LEGAL ENTITY?

As a company owner, it is in your best interest to get acquainted with every detail of your business and gain a thorough knowledge of how your company operates. On the other hand, no entrepreneur is, nor can be, an expert in every aspect of business and it is common to employ or consult experts, typically an accountant and a lawyer.

You may be hesitant when you think of their rather high remuneration or salary. But a skilful lawyer will save you a lot of angst and especially time, which you can invest in the development of your company and its profitability. Although it may not seem to be the case at the beginning, you'll be busy with everyday operations. You most likely will not have the time or thought capacity for studying all the new laws and decrees, not to mention continuously keeping up to date with their implementation in practice. The mistakes you could make would cost you dearly – even if you run just a small café or a button shop.

First of all, you need to find out if it is more convenient for you to run the business as a sole trader, that is a natural person (a self-employed individual who is in direct control of all elements and is legally accountable), or a legal entity (an association, corporation, partnership, proprietorship, trust or individual that has legal standing in the eyes of the law), and then you'll know what legislation will be binding for you. Of course, you can change your decision later on, but this change will incur certain complications and costs.

When deciding whether you're going to do business as a sole trader or establish a legal entity such as a limited company, you should take into account the following:

- Your specialization – if you make beautiful toys for children at home, you'll probably choose a different form of business than you would if you were to set up a PR agency.
- Your financial possibilities – the initial capital required and also the economic and administrative demand, which is higher in the case of a legal entity.

- Your appetite for risk – the extent of your liability for commitments that arise in connection with the business will vary depending on your field.
- The expected company development – if you're planning to have a partner or if you're thinking of selling the company in the future, it is better to be a legal entity.
- The size of the companies you want to work with – big companies sometimes don't like negotiating with self-employed individuals.

The undeniable advantage of self-employment is that you can often launch your business with very low initial investment. However, it may be a disadvantage to hold all financial and legal responsibility – you have nowhere to hide if trouble strikes, the buck stops with you.

"Originally I wanted to provide services as a tour operator, but I realized that as an anthropologist I didn't have the required qualification. I was supposed to find a guarantor. Unfortunately, I couldn't find anybody with the necessary credentials who would back me. In the end, after consulting a lawyer I decided to establish a travel agency, for which it is not necessary to meet any special requirements to obtain the relevant trade licence. An agency is not allowed to sell its own tours (but only work as an intermediary), but I often organize stays abroad for my clients, I buy plane tickets and book their accommodation. I must say I'm doing something I really like."

(Yvonne, 26, Hungary)

If being a sole trader doesn't suit your purposes, you still have the option to form a legal entity. The main advantage of this is the fact that the company's business assets are at risk, not the personal assets of the owners. Hence, this legal structure is chosen by people who run businesses that entail higher risk, or those applying for substantial loans. In conclusion, we can also say that a legal entity is suitable if there are several people doing business together and if you are going to trade with bigger or foreign corporations (who often view limited companies, for example, as being more trustworthy).

The forms of legal entities are in most countries **a joint-stock company** and **a limited liability company**. In some countries you can establish **public limited companies, limited partnerships** or **cooperatives**. In some cases it can be difficult to make the right decision, especially when you are unfamiliar with business law. By now it should be dawning on you why it is so important to consult with an expert on such important matters.

GET THE PERMITS

When you are setting up your business, depending on which country you are based in, you'll need to get the various licenses (and pay various fees) relevant to the industry you are entering. You can expect more intense regulation, for instance, in fields that involve handling food, selling alcohol or taking care of children. So if you're planning to open a private nursery school, you should expect to have to meet a lot of health and safety requirements and pass criminal checks.

It is highly likely that you will need licences in connection with your business – from the town hall, fire brigade, environmental health officer, conservationists and so on. Receiving one single "stamp" is usually subject to the condition of having a previous one, so it pays to find out right at the start in what order you need to apply for them. Local authorities can advise you and you should reserve enough time, and nerves, for carrying out the required tasks. Make sure that you don't forget anything, otherwise you risk penalties and sanctions for breaching regulations.

LOOSE LIPS SINK SHIPS

When entering into written agreements with suppliers and investors, don't forget to include a confidentiality clause that protects you from the risk that the person or company you're doing business with publishes or discloses sensitive information about you and your company to a third party. This may seem rather over the top to you, especially when you're just starting up your business, but you should bear in mind that not all entrepreneurs hold the same ethical code as you.

Imagine that on the occasion of the ceremonial opening you're planning to give a present to the first two hundred customers. You call the company that is supposed to deliver the gifts. Will you risk paying for those goods without having a confidentiality agreement in place, without any safeguard in case your supplier decides to disclose your intent to your competition? You should understand that an agreement isn't an expression of personal mistrust, but the protection of business interests – not only yours but also the other party's.

<hr>

"After I finished my studies, I decided to make use of the big garden behind our house by growing herbs to make natural cosmetics. At first, I sold my products mainly to my friends, but they recommended my products to other people – so I couldn't complain of being short of customers. One day a lady knocked on my door saying that she was very impressed with my cosmetics and wanted to work as a business representative for me. She claimed to know the market and have contacts. There was no reason why I shouldn't believe her, and after all a new group of clients always comes in handy. We agreed that at the end of each month she would bring me a list of companies she had visited and possibly sold something to. I was supposed to pay her a fixed salary in return. The first month everything went as it was supposed to, the following month there were some complications and after the salary for the third month went to her account she didn't call any more. It was a lesson learnt the hard way, and I'm sure that drawing up a cooperation contract with a lawyer would have cost me less than those three salaries."

(Odette, 26, France)

<hr>

WHAT CAN HAPPEN DAY-TO-DAY

Did you breathe a sigh of relief once your company was up and running? Do you have customers and your daily agenda and processes work as they should? That's nice, but you should keep in mind that the law and the taxman are never far away. You should still pay close attention to the following:

COMPANY DOCUMENTS

You need to ensure that your company works in accordance with its original commitments, which is why you must update all relevant documents (for instance company articles) whenever necessary.

LEGAL LIABILITY

There's always the risk that you'll have to face liability for debts, an employee injury at work or damage caused to a third person.

LEGISLATION RELATING TO LABOUR LAW

In most countries there is a range of legal regulations providing for relations between the employer and employee, and you need to be familiar with them before you actually hire your first employee. If you don't adhere to them, you risk big trouble.

LAWS ON INSURANCE

Your company may insure its liability, car fleet, property, transported goods and many other things. It pays to find out what must be insured and what insurance policies are optional. Although insurance companies will, of course, be pushing some of their products, in some cases you'd just be throwing money down the drain. By contrast, you should have a good insurance policy concerning liability, health and property/assets, duly updated and for adequate settlement amounts.

BUSINESS TERMS AND CONDITIONS

Precisely formulated business terms and conditions that clearly define the rights and obligations of your company to your customers and suppliers are necessary for everyone, not only for those running an e-shop, for example. They are important for everyone who provides services or goods to clients. I am sure you can recall a situation when you have signed a contract with an energy supplier, telephone operator or estate agency. Although the business terms and conditions may have been printed in fine type, they included essential information.

CHOOSING THE COMPANY LAWYER

Calculate whether it pays to cooperate with an external lawyer or to employ one. How often will you be using legal services? Whatever the case, you'll certainly need an erudite expert in business law, preferably one who specializes in small and medium-sized companies. But how can you find one?

- If you are unable to get a recommendation from your friends or peers, search on the Internet. Find the websites of lawyers and legal practices in your area whose specialization suits your needs and read through their profiles.

- Arrange to meet with a number of candidates. Most lawyers offer the first consultation for free, and after you meet them in person, it will be easier to decide which is the right one for you.

- Distinguish between advantageous and cheap offers. Don't base your decision primarily on money, however important it may be to you. You should compare price and "quality". If somebody offers services for low or below-average remuneration, it doesn't automatically mean you'll save money. On the contrary, incompetent advice can often deprive you of more money than consulting an "expensive" lawyer.

- Also take into account the human aspect of the lawyer you choose. A lawyer, just like an accountant, is crucial for your company, somebody you must trust completely.

BE CAREFUL AND DO YOUR PAPERWORK

We all make mistakes sometimes. Fortunately, we can often learn from the mistakes made by many entrepreneurs before us.

- If you haven't ruled out the possibility of future expansion into other countries, you should take a look at commercial registers abroad and check whether there is a company with a name identical or similar to yours.

- Be careful to whom and under what circumstances you provide your expert opinion, even if the other party may have requested it. There are people who enjoy seeking legal disputes, so it can easily happen that your good will won't pay off, as the counterparty may file a lawsuit trying to put the liability for their mistakes on you.

- Be cautious when doing business with your partner or friend. You might not want to bring law into a friendly relationship that works just fine. But it is exactly in such cases that a lawyer's intervention may help you set clear boundaries as to where your privacy ends and professional interests start. It will facilitate your cooperation and you can prevent possible complications. In the case of any discrepancies, you may not save your relationship, but you can preserve your joint business.

- Find a way to avoid clients who refuse to pay. No entrepreneurs can avoid defaulters, so you should carefully consider to whom you're going to deliver your goods or services "on credit". You may request payment before or upon delivery of the goods.

- Keep an eye on what kind of information leaves your company, whether it is purely business matters or information about you. Not everyone needs to know your mobile phone number, where you live or where your children go to school.

- Document most of what is going on in your company. Don't worry, I am not suggesting that you should simply be suspicious of everyone. However, if a problem arises, this documentation will come in handy either as background material for somebody else (inspection from the tax office, etc.) or for your own use if you want to discover the root cause of a problem.
- Be ready to settle problems with your employees correctly and in accordance with relevant legal regulations. It may happen that you'll need to dismiss somebody or that you receive notice of resignation from an employee. You should always document any disagreements with your employees. What it always comes down to is a good agreement that covers all aspects of the labour law relationship between the employer and employee.
- Have watertight agreements with all your suppliers and employees. It may sound like a banal remark, but, believe it or not, it's not always common practice. You should be aware that even the nicest colleagues from whom you wouldn't expect any dishonest behaviour at all, can later turn out to be cheaters and thieves who deprive you of your money or good reputation without batting an eyelid.

Although you're not a lawyer and you've already found a specialist, try to have at least a rough idea of the legal matters concerning establishing and running your company.

DON'T LIVE IN FEAR OF THE TAX OFFICE

Now is the time to get acquainted with taxes and accounting. I agree that dealing with taxes and company finances is not great fun. It is a necessity; we could call it a "tax for doing business". If you want to run your own business, you'll need to tackle this issue, whether you like it or not. As a company owner, and probably also an employer, you are responsible for timely payment of taxes, which is something you didn't have to think or care about when you were an employee. Remember that the government doesn't only want you to calculate the taxes due, but also to report them and pay them on time. If you omit anything, you'll be charged potentially high penalties and default interest.

"Two years after I started my own business I went on holiday with my family and our neighbours flooded us out. It was a big shock when we returned. Unfortunately, besides having our furniture and other furnishings destroyed, we also lost our family photographs and personal documents. As if that were not enough, all my accounting documents were destroyed too. What followed was agony. The tax office, where I reported the loss, recommended that I try to get hold of all these documents again. So the following month I spent endless hours on the phone and visiting companies I traded with asking them to find the relevant payments and invoices. In the end, I succeeded in getting everything and submitted my tax return in time. But I wouldn't wish on anyone the sleepless nights I had when I was afraid of the big fine that was hanging above me like the sword of Damocles."
(Sophia, 34, USA)

This book cannot provide specific information on this topic since tax regulations are different in every country. However, if you tend to handle most matters concerning your business yourself, you should consider making an exception when it comes to taxes and accounting (as we're going to explain later on). The decision to hire an appropriate tax advisor will save you a lot of money and you'll avoid the risk of making a mistake and having to pay fines. An accountant will certainly know how to prepare your accounts so that you don't pay more than is really necessary. Thanks to this expert advice, you'll thus keep more of the money you earn.

Mistakes in income tax returns cost entrepreneurs a lot of money each year, regardless of whether they calculate taxes themselves or with the help of an accountant. I don't mean to cast any aspersions on accountants, but I'd like to point out how vast a topic taxes is and that the legislation keeps changing almost every year. Moreover, dealing with taxes is not only restricted to filling in your tax return and submitting it. A tax advisor will help you most when you consult your strategic plans. They can outline for you how a certain intention will influence your taxes, so you'll have the chance to steer the company in another direction if your original idea is disadvantageous.

A TAX ADVISOR IS NOT THE SAME AS AN ACCOUNTANT

What we have already said about tax advisors also applies to accountants. You may be thinking that, although accounting is a complex issue, it cannot be that complicated for a small company. If you are still hesitant about whether it is necessary to spend money on accounting services (whether working for you externally or as an employee), you should realize that good accountants will not only maintain the accounts, but they can also take care of the finances for your entire company.

- They will advise you as to which legal form best suits your needs from the perspective of money and taxes.
- They won't fully replace a tax advisor, but they can help you with taxes in general.
- They will make sure you don't mix up your personal and business costs.
- They will help you with various business transactions.
- They will provide you with a financial statement for every accounting period.
- They will analyse the financial statement and advise you how to make better financial decisions in the future.

Each professional accountant has to know the current version of ever-changing laws and legal regulations, so they'll save you energy and time that you would otherwise have to expend in an effort to understand the relevant legislation, while also absorbing regular new amendments. It is reasonable to delegate these tasks to an expert in order to save yourself the trouble and invest your efforts into the business itself.

"I studied at an economics college, so I boasted that I could certainly do without an accountant. Moreover, I only ran a small decorating studio, so I believed I wouldn't have to do much paperwork anyway. A typical beginner's mistake: that's what I'm saying today. Of course, I soon got immersed in running the studio, so I did accounting as and

when I needed to. I didn't have the time to study new laws, decrees and regulations, but I still didn't want to give it up. I only came around after I made a fatal mistake when calculating my tax, for which the tax office gave me a stiff fine. These days I cooperate with a great accountant and I swear by her. "

(Ulrike, 33, Germany)

FIND AN ACCOUNTANT WITH A GOOD TRACK RECORD

If you want to find a good accountant, you should first ask your friends for a recommendation. Then search for references that attest not only to professional qualities, but also personal traits. You certainly won't benefit from collaborating with someone who'll disappear one day with your company money. And you don't need a newly qualified eager beaver who has less experience than you require. You're searching for a reliable and qualified professional.

When choosing your accountant focus mainly on the following:

- Do you need an accountant to keep your accounts including salaries and taxes? Then you should be doubly careful. Not every accountant focuses on taxes and salaries. There are some accountants who only specialize in salaries, while some only do accounting (without doing salaries).

- The expert you choose should be able to give you advice in all financial matters – how to increase your cash flow, cope with your creditors and collect due receivables.

- It is advisable to pick somebody who is familiar with all relevant regulations concerning employment.

- Make sure that the applicant is able to interlink his or her knowledge and provide you with an analysis if you need it about, for instance, the expected growth, cash flow or ratio between your debts and income, depreciations and so on.
- It will certainly come in handy if the candidate you choose knows his or her way around company funding. You may reach a point when you need to take out a loan, which means you'll need to have somebody reliable and experienced by your side who will guide you through the process of searching for the most suitable way of funding.

QUESTIONS TO CONSIDER

AM I GOING TO WORK WITH AN EXTERNAL LAWYER, OR DOES IT PAY TO EMPLOY A COMPANY LAWYER?

Consider to what extent you can keep the lawyer occupied and make your decision accordingly.

HAVE I FOUND A LAWYER WITH THE SPECIALIZATION I NEED?

You need to know what it is exactly that you're going to request from your lawyer.

HAVE I MADE IT CLEAR WHAT I EXPECT FROM MY ACCOUNTANT?

Not all accountants have the same professional scope.

HAVE I SUCCEEDED IN FINDING THE RIGHT EXPERT?

You need a qualified expert you can absolutely rely on.

Chapter 10

The power of brand

Even the best product or service won't do without a well-thought-out brand and image

When you hear the words "shop front", you probably imagine a small shop with a striped awning and colourful flower pots at the entrance. In fact, there's much more to it. If you have a brick-and-mortar shop, the image doesn't only concern what your shop physically looks like, but also how your customers perceive you or your brand and how you sell your products or services. The same applies to selling online where the shop front is your e-shop design and the image of your brand.

However, a brand is not just a logo on your product packaging. It is something that exists in customers' minds and emotions. Brands are what lead customers to perceive that your product has something extra in addition to its basic functions and they strongly influence customer behaviour.

Building a brand is a long-distance run. You should be ready to make an array of decisions in this respect. After all, the slightest detail, such as the colour you use on your company pens or the music that plays in your shop or beauty salon, is of great importance. All of this influences your image and how your customers will perceive you. So let's take a closer look at what influences customer perception, from branding to customer experience.

A BRAND IS WHAT YOU'RE LEFT WITH EVEN IF YOUR SHOP BURNS DOWN

Let's play a little game. Read the brief descriptions of well-known brands and try to guess which companies they refer to. Ready? Steady. Go!

1) Two golden arches forming the letter M.

2) An apple with a bite taken out of it.

3) A swoosh.

4) A logo with two overlapping mirror-like letter Cs.

5) Four silver circles in a row linked together.

Did you know them all? The answers are: 1) McDonald's, 2) Apple, 3) Nike, 4) Chanel and 5) Audi. Even if you didn't recognize all of them, you'll know what they have in common.

These companies are known worldwide. Why? Because they have succeeded in building an incredibly strong brand. A brand so famous that people identify it just by seeing its logo or hearing its slogan.

A brand is just as important for small and medium-sized businesses, which is why you need to focus on it right from the start and build it continually. A brand is one of the most effective weapons in fighting the competition, and the stronger it is, the less it is jeopardized by rivals or market fluctuations. A brand tempts customers to try out the product. Its power creates a strong emotional bond between the customer and the brand. It decides who is going to be the market leader.

When advertising agencies or marketing managers build a brand, they focus on so-called branding. What is it? Many people would say it is simply a symbol, logo, colour or combination of these aspects, by which we distinguish one company from another. However, there are really many elements that are part of branding: some are visible to you, others are perceived only subliminally. In principle, the point is that anyone who comes across anything that is related to your business should be able to identify the brand. It can be a certain style, distinctive logo, a slogan that gets under your skin, a colour that is typical of your brand – for instance, the pink colour used by T-Mobile. Even the cushions in relaxation rooms for T-Mobile employees are that specific dark shade of pink.

In other words, whatever you do it must represent your brand at all times – both inside and outside of your company, across your customers, suppliers and employees.

Since a brand is an inseparable part of your company, and it will be everywhere, it is crucial to think carefully about what it should be like and what it should represent.

Your brand should:
- Motivate customers to buy and facilitate their decision-making process
- Enhance their loyalty
- Evoke emotions
- Increase the company's trustworthiness
- Clearly and comprehensively convey your message to customers

HOW TO BUILD A STRONG BRAND

Consider what you want people to think of when they hear your company name. What values should be linked to your brand? Seriousness? Playfulness? Friendliness? High quality? Tradition? Modernity? It is important to know this, as it has an impact on all aspects of your company.

How to build the right brand

- Simplicity is beauty. The simpler the name, the easier it will be for people to remember. Make sure it can be easily pronounced and spelled so that your customers will be able to find you more easily.

- The company name and the brand must both somehow express the essence of your business. Maybe you want your brand to evoke customers' emotions and be identified immediately. Look at BBC Radio, Costa Coffee and Bet365 – their names immediately tell you what they offer. For instance, Benetton built its brand on the family name of the owners, and it succeeded in building such brand awareness (in a rather short time) that you immediately know what the company does. The name is linked with the above-mentioned playfulness, vigour and courage, and its owners are not afraid of making fun of themselves, which pays off when building the brand. Nothing ventured, nothing gained. The brand is getting more and more famous and stronger, and the company is outgrowing its competition.

- Your brand must be consistent. Building a brand takes years, as does keeping it relevant. It is linked with rather substantial investment, so it is not possible to easily change the brand name, style, communication, slogan or corporate colours. That would effectively mean a fresh start for your company.

- A brand needs to be protected. The moment you finalize what it will look like, you should register it as a trademark with the Intellectual Property Office (IPO). A trademark is covered for ten years, and it's certainly not worth risking somebody stealing or copying it from you. A brand is your family silver and it requires the utmost care.

From her entrepreneurial beginnings running a catering service in the cellar of her home, Martha Stewart worked her way up to having her own TV show, publishing several cookery books, launching an online magazine and establishing her own production company. Despite accusations of shady financial manoeuvres, she managed to successfully return to her business. "Martha Stewart managed to build a personal brand that everybody is receptive to and knows well. It is her name that sells and opens doors for her throughout various segments", states an article on Lupa.cz. "A common American woman links the Martha Stewart brand to wine, furniture, a TV programme and a book. We could hardly find someone else like this who has built a brand out of nothing that sells so well." (14)

GIVE YOUR BRAND A FACE

Your brand is slowly coming into existence and it is time to get the nursery ready. What do you actually need in order for your brand to finally be born?

- Business name
- Corporate colours
- Logo
- Slogan
- Company font

Unless you're keen on graphic design and are used to working with graphic software, you should entrust an expert with creating a logo and visual identity for your brand. These days it is child's play to find a graphic designer who will create a custom logo including colour composition for company catalogues, business cards or printing on your office supplies.

Where will your brand name in the form of your logo appear? Everywhere! For example:

- Websites
- Print advertising
- Social media
- Blogs
- Elsewhere on the Internet (e.g. in search results, banners, PR articles)
- A shop or place visited by your customers
- Product packaging
- Business cards
- Promotional stands
- Advertising materials (e.g. posters, leaflets, catalogues)
- Promotional items

Everything relating to your company and every business activity you carry out must reflect elements of your company style. Everything you produce should bear your logo, your corporate colours, the same font and uniform design.

IMAGE IS A CHALLENGE FOR THE ENTIRE COMPANY

Image is linked with success. Does your brand have the potential to create the right image? You should realize that it is going to appear everywhere and may be linked to your company forever, so it must aptly depict the desired image of your company.

So what should your company image be like? Try to answer the following questions and you'll get the answer.

- Is my company serious, formal, solemn, humorous, mysterious, childlike/playful, feminine, masculine, whacky, dynamic...? Pick one word that best describes what impression your company should leave and keep it in mind when creating the brand.

- What do I want people to think of when they see my brand, meaning what particular thought or feeling should it evoke.
- What colours should I use for my logo? As is well known, different colours evoke different emotions. Red represents passion, fire and strong will. Green is reminiscent of expensive things, ecology, luxury and money. The colour blue is calming, quiet and tranquil. Yellow reflects positives, as it represents happiness, light and sun. Orange is warm and pleasant. In order to pick the right colour, study in depth what feelings each colour evokes and then choose the right one for you.

Marketing research says that up to 80 per cent of the visual information we receive is connected with colours. More precisely, it is colours that send us certain communications. As the psychoanalyst Carl Gustav Jung said, colours are the native language of our sub-consciousness … Have you noticed that most fast food restaurants use red, orange or yellow? That's because they know these colours stimulate diners to eat quickly. Eat up and go. (15)

What colours have famous brands picked?
- **Red** appears in the logos of Coca-Cola, Kit Kat, Red Cross and Vodafone.
- **Blue** dominates brands such as Peugeot, Volkswagen, O2 and IBM.
- **Green** was chosen by the makers of the TV channel Animal Planet and the Android operation system.

- **Yellow** is the colour of Nikon and the world-famous movie database IMDb.
- **Orange** is dominant in the logo of phone operator Orange and the Firefox web browser.

Do you know how you're going to present you brand? You need to bear this in mind all the time. If you choose the wrong image at the beginning, you'll feel the consequences over and over again. It won't be easy to change it, just as it is not easy to alter the first impression you leave with people. Each detail plays a role and everything must gel and support your business targets.

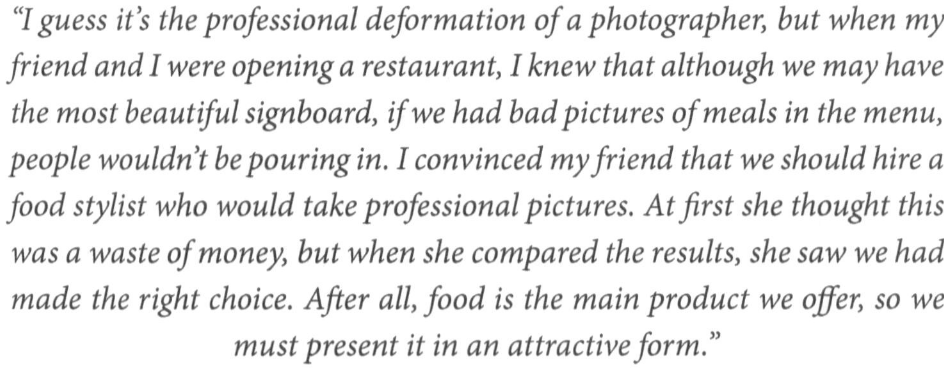

"I guess it's the professional deformation of a photographer, but when my friend and I were opening a restaurant, I knew that although we may have the most beautiful signboard, if we had bad pictures of meals in the menu, people wouldn't be pouring in. I convinced my friend that we should hire a food stylist who would take professional pictures. At first she thought this was a waste of money, but when she compared the results, she saw we had made the right choice. After all, food is the main product we offer, so we must present it in an attractive form."

(Clara, 37, USA)

SHOPPING MUST BE A GREAT EXPERIENCE FOR YOUR CUSTOMER

It doesn't matter if you're selling goods in a brick-and-mortar shop or on the Internet. It is important to attract people and create an appealing shopping environment. Think about your own shopping experiences. Imagine you're entering a shop that sells costume jewellery and you don't know where to look first – earrings, bracelets and necklaces are beautifully lit and arranged so that the colours and materials are coordinated. Then you go to a nearby competitor where all the goods lie around in tasteless plastic baskets, often even packed in plastic bags. Who are you going to buy from? Certainly from the shop with a pleasant environment where you feel relaxed and enjoy your shopping experience.

Find a way to give your customers a good experience. If you have a brick-and-mortar shop:

- Make sure everything is well lit and visible.
- All your goods must be accessible and clearly arranged.
- Your shop windows must attract attention, captivate and evoke desire. Research shows that passers-by look in a shop window for three to seven seconds. During this time, customers decide whether they will or won't enter the shop. Convince them with a well-planned and inventive display.

If you have an e-shop:

- When customers shop online, they choose mainly with their eyes just as they do in brick-and-mortar shops, so photographs of the products must be of good quality and appealing.
- An e-shop should be clearly arranged so that customers can easily navigate through it.

Attractive presentation is very important for any kind of goods or services. You should thus devote enough time to it and not skimp on the details as they often prove to be a decisive factor in where people shop.

The Internet has one disadvantage. When shopping online, customers cannot examine the goods carefully, touch them or try them out. This means that the attractive presentation of a product or service is even more important in the case of an e-shop. You need to arouse desire in customers to buy the given thing and give them a reason to do it. Photographs should be of good quality and the product should be depicted realistically. Help your customers choose the right thing – if you're selling, say, clothes, don't show dresses on hangers or tossed on the table; display them in photographs being worn by real models. Arrange jewels so that they look even more luxurious. Let your imagination run wild.

DO YOU KNOW WHAT YOUR CUSTOMER EXPECTS?

Can you really satisfy your customer's fantasies and needs? Another thing you must understand is what your customers' expectations are. Your brand gives them the information you want to communicate, but you also need to focus on communication in the opposite direction: from the client to you. What does your customer really need? And how can you find out?

Start by looking at the competition, especially at big companies with a wide customer portfolio. As they're successful on the market, they know what customers expect. They usually have an understanding of client needs that is founded on research and many years of experience from which you can profit. Naturally, you can imitate them (that is cheap), but you can also get inspired and learn from what these companies have already tried.

It is also a good idea to work with empathy. Try to feel what your customer feels. Think about what you expect when you're shopping for clothes, going to an Italian restaurant or for a pedicure, for example, or when you're attending dance lessons. Answering these questions may help you clarify the message your business should be communicating to your customers.

However, expectations are not only important during an actual shopping experience, you also need to know what your clients expect when they come to your website or follow you on Facebook. All of this forms their brand experience. If that experience is positive, your customers will be happy to share it. And you can take my word for it, positive references work like an aphrodisiac. Can there be anything better than having crowds of people who long for what you're offering? This has been achieved, for instance, by Apple, where demand often exceeds supply, or IKEA – just think how many people are delighted when they find an IKEA catalogue in their mailbox. That's why you should focus on customer service too. People want to be spoilt; they want to have their needs and wishes satisfied. You should see this as a challenge to be met.

QUESTIONS TO CONSIDER

WHAT WILL BE MY BRAND IMAGE?

Write down anything that comes to your mind. It can be an idea about your logo or slogan that will express the essence of your business or a detail concerning your point of sale. Actually put down all your thoughts.

WHAT COLOURS, FONTS AND MOTIFS WILL I USE?

Remember that all of these elements make up your image, so it is important to think twice before making a decision.

WHAT WILL I CALL MY COMPANY?

Be creative, but pick a name that will be simple, effective and easy to remember.

HOW WILL I PRESENT MY PRODUCTS OR SERVICES?

Think about how you could address your potential customers and, above all, how to catch their interest.

WHAT IMAGE DO I WANT TO HAVE AND HOW CAN I ACHIEVE IT?

It is enormously important that the image of your company really reflects the fundamentals of your business on all fronts, including the values your company holds and wants to present to the world. You should really think carefully about this.

WHAT ARE MY CUSTOMERS' EXPECTATIONS?

Why should the customer decide to buy my particular service or product? Would I choose it if I were in their place?

Chapter 11

How to get under your customer's skin?

Marketing is too important to be left to the marketing department (Dave Packard)

Has it ever occurred to you that great companies own great brands and great brands belong to great companies? This is almost always the case, so it is no coincidence. You may ask what companies actually have brands for. Without them they would be churning out products of the same quality and would only be competing on price. Brands enhance their ability to create profit, as they can significantly influence consumer behaviour and entice people to try their product. Raising consumers' interest in products and services is the task of marketing. No entrepreneur starts doing business without the prospect of profit: however, this may come only when people know what you're offering, no matter if your goods are paper fold-up toys or spare parts for agricultural machines. They'll only learn after you start promoting your products and services. The question is how to do it.

Every company, without exception, however it functions, can benefit from marketing campaigns and higher brand awareness, win more clients, increase its sales and thus its profits. With a campaign, you're telling the world you exist, you're building your brand and increasing awareness. A campaign can support your products, accentuate their advantages, attract new customers and freeze out your competition. It doesn't matter how brilliant your products or services are, you definitely need marketing, because without it you'll be left standing still and the company won't develop or grow. The market will stop being interested in you; you won't gain new customers or build your business. Surely you don't want this? Therefore, you should try to find the best way to strengthen your business. What should you start with?

MARKETING STRATEGY VERSUS MARKETING PLAN

People often mistake a marketing strategy for a marketing plan and vice versa, although the difference is quite apparent. A marketing strategy defines the targets you want to achieve via marketing (these should naturally stem from your business goals, so your business goals and marketing strategy should go hand in hand). Your marketing strategy outlines what you want to achieve, whereas your marketing plan defines how you're going to achieve it: your marketing plan actually implements your marketing strategy. Many entrepreneurs try to skip to HOW without knowing WHAT and they thus start with their marketing plan. Naturally, this leads to wasting time and company finances.

Marketing strategy + marketing plan + implementation = **SUCCESS**

MARKETING STRATEGY

Your marketing strategy should contain the following:
- Company vision and mission
- Short-term objectives
- Long-term objectives

- Situation on the market (market share, competition analysis, threats, advantages, weaknesses, potential = SWOT analysis)
- Brand shaping – its position on the market, its characteristics
- Short description of the products or services that will be supported by marketing, and their advantages
- Description of your target customer – who the campaign will be aimed at

Preparing your marketing strategy is crucial. Just like with anything else, even here you can do it yourself – after all, you know your company better than anyone else. You can, of course, find an expert – a strategist who will do it for you. In the second case, you should thoroughly prepare because you'll need to define the assignment and your expectations in great detail, or you'll have to cooperate very closely with the expert.

MARKETING PLAN

Once you have your marketing strategy, you can plan specific marketing activities that will help you meet the targets you set. You should create a marketing plan every year and update it as needed according to the market and your company.

When making your marketing plan, you should bear in mind that the planning process is just as important as the plan itself. Behind a plan on two sheets of A4 paper there may be many hours of work. The plan reflects, in a way, your expectations of the future and this "future model" should be based on the right assumptions and define the route to your future vision. If you omit any of the important factors, work from wrong assumptions or if your targets and processes don't tie in with your plan, anything you plan won't work.

Try to use the budget you have for marketing the most efficiently. Each company defines this budget differently. In some companies it is a certain percentage of the income of the previous period, in others it is determined according to the results of marketing activities in the previous year and using up any remnants of the previous budget. There are many options. It is important to assess all previous marketing activities so that you are positive that the money you have invested has indeed achieved the desired result and is being used effectively.

Experience shows that in times of crisis, marketing is one of the first areas where companies start saving and cut their budgets. That is the wrong strategy – especially as these budgets are often undervalued or completely restricted anyway. Marketing directly influences a company's profits and it is crucial in crises.

DO YOU KNOW IF IT HAS PAID OFF?

In order to be able to assess how effective your marketing activities are, you need to evaluate them on a regular basis. That's why you first need to set particular targets for your campaigns and other activities. They must be specific, measurable, attainable, realistic and time bound – SMART.

Examples of specific targets include:
- Signing a certain number of contracts in the period January–June.
- Increasing your production by a certain number or percentage in a given period.
- Growth in new customer numbers by a certain percentage or a specified number.
- Improving customer retention.

- Increasing your turnover, net profit or sales of a certain product by a certain number or percentage.
- Increasing your website's conversion rate – for instance, increasing the number of completed order forms from three to ten a day or by a certain percentage.

To assess the ROI you may use a simple formula which can also be applied elsewhere, not only in marketing. This formula expresses the difference between the money invested and earned. Therefore, it shows you the profit as a percentage of the amount invested.

$$\text{ROI (in \%)} = \text{profit} / \text{investment} \times 100$$

- **What will you get?**

You'll see immediately whether your investment has paid off. It is easiest to count its return from the start of the campaign, because it allows you to set the ideal value of your investment and monitor it during the campaign (not only after it ends) – if the campaign doesn't give you the expected result, there's still time for you to make adjustments.

For example, let's say you have an average of five customers a day, each of them paying you £50, in your beauty salon. You decide to launch a radio campaign costing £150,000. If only five new customers arrive, then you've clearly not chosen an efficient communication tool. At first sight it may seem that your campaign worked, because the number of your customers has increased. In reality, however, the money you make cannot even cover the campaign costs, let alone any extra profit. Naturally, you may see a campaign as also being an investment in brand building, but next time you should choose a more efficient communication tool for promoting your business – for instance, an online campaign or PR campaign that may be partially free.

"I always saw marketing as a kind of bothersome discipline that forces sellers to offer customers any old thing, even though they may not actually need it. Before I started to run my own business, it had never occurred to me that putting a display board up with a name on it next to my flower shop or selling flowers at a discount in the last hour before closing is marketing. I came to understand that you cannot do business without having good products, just as you cannot do business without good marketing."
(Grace, 37, UK)

What tools can you work with in your marketing plan? Let's have a look at marketing mix.

MARKETING MIX IS NOT JUST ADVERTISING

A set of tools called a marketing mix is an important aspect of a marketing plan. People often think this term refers to advertising, but that is just a part of it. A traditional marketing mix consists of the so-called 5Ps:

1. PRODUCT

Product is what matters as it is the medium of exchange. Differences between products are physical as well as psychological:

- Physical differences
- Differences in availability
- Differences in service
- Price differences
- Differences in image

What does that mean in practice? Imagine a customer standing in a shop next to a sandwich display. Among the selection of sandwiches are some made in your deli. The customer is hungry, but it is quite possible that he or she will reach for one of your competitor's products simply because it has attracted his or her attention with more durable or attractive packaging. In marketing we speak of the so-called three-layer concept of a product, where other decisive aspects of purchase are in addition to the product itself, its quality, design and the image of the manufacturer, packaging and accompanying services such as installation, time of delivery, settling of complaints and so on.

2. PRICE

The price is the exchange value expressed in money, and a discount is an adjustment to the ratio between quality and price. However, pricing policy doesn't simply lie in setting the price. While some companies sell at fixed prices, that is prices from a set price list, others often use discounts, reliefs, benefits and systems of instalments and loans (e.g. a car bought through leasing, a flat bought with a mortgage etc.).

People like discounts and most of all they like getting things for free, and although at the beginning your company won't have money to spare, it would be short-sighted of you not to use this fact to your advantage, at least from time to time. Naturally, it is important to calculate whether it will pay to decrease your prices or invest in giving out gifts. Time-limited offers work perfectly; on the other hand, decreasing your prices may be quite risky. That's why you should also look at these decisions from a long-term perspective. Pricing policies based on decreasing your prices constantly and long-term strategies aimed at being the cheapest seller on the market are sure-fire ways to disaster from where there is no return. Therefore, you should think twice before you make any price reductions.

Short-term offers should be linked to a certain time of the year, festivals or public holidays (e.g. Valentine's Day) or another event (e.g. an anniversary). You may offer discounts on certain days of the year or give out presents for free to a certain number of customers who buy something from you. Each event will attract customers' attention. For instance:

- The Easter Bunny is bringing presents! Get a 20 per cent discount on your order – only this weekend!
- Help us celebrate our first anniversary. We will reward every shopper with a small gift.
- Recommend us. Bring a new customer and you'll get a 50 per cent discount on one item.
- Grand opening celebration – the first 500 customers will receive a gift from us!
- Spend more than £100 online and we'll deliver to your doorstep for free.
- Every fifth customer wins a prize! First x number of customers win!

There are many possibilities; let your imagination run wild. Advertise your special offers at your brick-and-mortar shop, on your website and on social media.

3. PLACE

Distribution is:

- Transporting goods from the manufacturer to the customer
- Availability (accessibility) of the product
- Atmosphere and position of the shop

How are you going to get your product or service to your end customer? Whether your business succeeds or fails is dependent upon the availability of the product or service you offer. For example, there is a big difference between offering your goat's milk yoghurt just on your farm and making it available in supermarkets, at farmer's markets and also in some smaller shops all around the country. The distribution category includes the distribution network, delivery and transport. To cut a long story short, there are many factors that have an impact on how successful your business will be and none of them should be underestimated.

4. PROMOTION

Promotion is the most visible part of the marketing mix. It deals with the promotion of goods and services and, according to US marketing guru Philip Kotler, it includes, in addition to advertising (the most significant part), **sales support, personal selling, direct marketing and PR**.

- **Sales promotions**

  This represents things that prompt the customer to buy goods and it typically concerns pricing (discounts, buy two get one free, etc.). But sales promotions can have many other formats: presentation of the goods at the place with highest concentration of target customers, tastings, trial specimens, vouchers, contests for customers and prize draw competitions, time-limited offers, product location in a shop (e.g. attractive stands at the cash desks), member-ship in the customers' club, system of discounts or vouch-ers, gift items, benefits for important customers (discount cards, cinema tickets, cheaper sports activities), publish-ing company magazines with practical information, recipes, discount vouchers and many others. All you need to do is to pick the one most relevant to your business.

- **Personal selling**

  Presenting products to prospective buyers "face to face" is the most effective and also the most expensive tool for sellers. In this case, an individual salesperson sells a product or ser-vice to a client. Either the seller and potential purchaser know each other or they've met on recommendation from a mutual acquaintance – the customer. Personal selling often involves the development of longstanding relationships between the salesperson and the client. For example, a salesperson in a furniture show room sells directly to the consumer who walks in off the street; a distributor for a brand that uses the multi-level marketing principle, such as Avon or Oriflame cosmet-ics, sells to someone on their doorstep. The same applies in a business to business situation. For example, a manufacturer of hospital equipment relies on sales reps to sell their products to medical practices; a food producer employs sales reps to meet with wholesale or retail buyers to convince them to stock their goods. Watch out! Don't mistake personal selling for other business practices such as mail order, telesales, selling at exhibitions and fairs and so on.

- **Direct marketing**

Direct marketing includes several forms of promotion, ranging from sending marketing messages by mail (letters with advantageous offers, catalogues, leaflets and mass mail drops) to communication on the phone (telemarketing and mobile marketing) to emailing (sending offers and promotions, including newsletters, electronically). Email is probably the most frequently used method these days due to low costs, time flexibility and potential for precise monitoring and evaluation.

However, a good and regularly updated database of email contacts is a prerequisite. Creating one may take some time, but it pays off. Of course, you can also buy such a database, but you'll always be running the risk that a substantial number of the email addresses are non-active, which means you'll be paying for worthless addresses. Also, a great number of recipients will have never heard of you and certainly don't intend to buy anything from you. It is very hard to check the quality of a database before you actually buy it.

One of the ways in which you can start generating your own database is to place a form on your website via which users may sign up to receive your newsletter. Offer them this possibility also on social media and in your email signature ("sign up to receive our newsletter at www.mycompany.co.uk"). You will then be able to inform a great number of people about your company news and special offers.

How can you compile a newsletter so that recipients notice it in the flood of information they receive and don't just delete it with a single click? Captivate them! You have one second before the recipient decides whether to open or delete your email. It is thus important to first catch their attention in the subject line and then with an attractive and pleasantly formatted newsletter. You should view the text of the email through the eyes of the recipient. Each newsletter should include answers to the following questions:

- Who's writing to me?
- What do they want?
- Why should I care?
- What is in it for me?
- What should I do?

You should focus on the subject of the message, which should tempt the recipient to open the email, while not giving everything away.

This text should be informal (but not too familiar), and bear in mind that people are overloaded with information these days and they have little time, so it is important to get straight to the point. The information you send must have value. If you're running a flower shop, write about flowers that are fashionable right now, about the meaning of different kinds of flowers or the latest trends in colours for weddings. Keep focused on what you want to tell the world (e.g. draw attention to a timelimited discount for wedding flowers). Prompt your readers to immediate action (register, sign up, etc.), otherwise you risk them immediately forgetting about it.

Pay attention to graphic layout. This can instantly "kill" interest, no matter how fascinating it may be. It is a good idea to ask a graphic designer to make a simple newsletter template instead of having to write everything in the body of a new email.

Watch out for the selection and size of photographs and how they are presented!

Don't send your newsletter more often than once every two weeks, or – even better – once a month, otherwise you risk the recipients feeling overwhelmed with your marketing materials and never reading them. Or, even worse, they'll unsubscribe from receiving your newsletter and you won't get them back.

Remember that unsolicited mail is spam and spamming is prohibited. So you should only send your newsletter to those who have given you their consent with a subscription. Don't forget to include in your newsletter the option to unsubscribe. This is required by law and, if you fail to do so, you risk heavy penalties.

- **Advertising campaigns**
  Advertising campaigns may take different forms depending on the objective, target audience, product, type of company and timing. Advertising aimed at elderly people offering them a tour, for example, will look different from an advertisement promoting student bank accounts and totally different again from a promotion for nappies. The objective of an advertising campaign is very important and this will vary. The intention could be to introduce a product to the market, highlight a special offer, increase brand awareness, build up the company image, increase sales or perhaps to retain customers.

TV commercials are intended for mass audiences and, since they require the investment of many millions, they are used mainly by large enterprises. The situation is similar with radio stations and national newspapers. Advertising in traditional nationwide, or even global, media is generally very expensive and it only pays off for those companies that need to have wide coverage and can afford to promote their products or services on an ongoing basis. However, there's nothing standing in your way if you want to advertise in local periodicals or on regional TV channels where prices are more favourable. These media are suitable for entrepreneurs with local focus who only need to reach a select part of the general public in a specific location. If you've opened a furniture shop on a square in your town, for example, you should certainly consider this option. The situation is different if you run an e-shop selling gardening tools. You'll probably reach customers most effectively if you advertise in a specialist magazine and combine it with advertising on the Internet. A specialist magazine will have a smaller print run but, thanks to its focus, the audience will include a higher number of people interested in gardening than a regional TV channel, radio station or newspaper. This also applies to specialist websites. So, you should always keep in mind the relevance and target audience.

As for **print media**, there is also a whole range of regional catalogues and directories of companies and services that are distributed for free. However, their distribution network and the target market they approach also need to be considered. This form of advertising certainly isn't advantageous for all entrepreneurs.

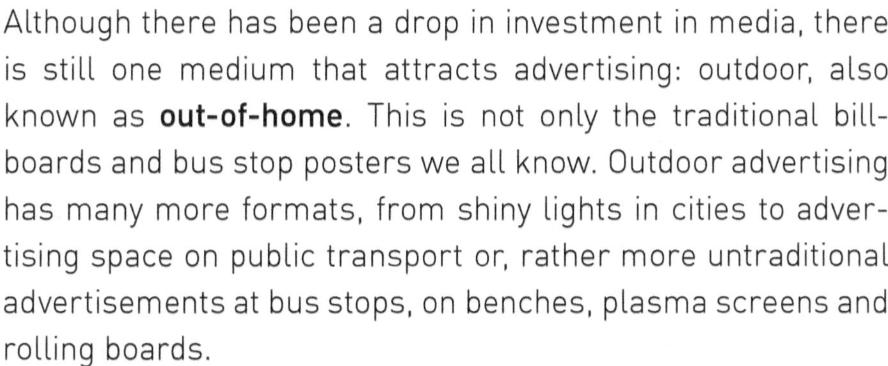

"I was working as a bus driver, but my passion was cooking. I cooked for my children; I cooked for my husband; I cooked for my relatives and friends. But after twenty years we had a crisis. We divorced, our sons were grown up and I didn't know how to go on. Once they said to me: 'Mum, why don't you fly with us to New Zealand to pick apples?' At first I thought they were crazy, but then I realized it was not a bad idea. As soon as the farm owner found out I knew my way around the kitchen, he charged me with making food for the workers. Then, when he was eating with us one time, he enjoyed it so much that he offered me a job in his restaurant. Later on I found myself a new husband and helped James, the restaurant owner, to open another restaurant. In order to be a good boss, I started studying marketing textbooks. It is nice that I can immediately try out ideas in my role to find out what works for people."
(Ilona, 46, New Zealand)

Although there has been a drop in investment in media, there is still one medium that attracts advertising: outdoor, also known as **out-of-home**. This is not only the traditional billboards and bus stop posters we all know. Outdoor advertising has many more formats, from shiny lights in cities to advertising space on public transport or, rather more untraditional advertisements at bus stops, on benches, plasma screens and rolling boards.

The general public are bombarded with advertisements and people are often "blind" to traditional media – hence there is less and less attention being paid to this form of advertising. Therefore, it is important to come up with new ways to successfully reach your target audience. Outdoor is a three-second medium, so what counts here is creativity, innovation, striking power and simplicity. Just think how much time you can spend "studying" this advertising space while you're driving. If you don't spot something immediately, you don't see it at all. You should bear this in mind if you decide to invest in an outdoor advertising campaign. Outdoor is most suitable for so-called image advertising, that is, campaigns aimed at building or raising brand awareness.

As for the aforementioned media investment, the only medium advertisers are putting more money into is the Internet, even during crises. Yes, we're talking about online advertising, which also boasts the highest flexibility, efficiency and measurability. A huge amount of communication is taking place online these days – there are increasingly more and more users, technology keeps developing and relatively low costs allow even small companies or start-ups to let the world know they exist. Moreover, online advertising allows for quite precise targeting and flexible response (if the response is not in accordance with your expectations, you can modify your campaign or stop it).

One great advantage of online marketing is the availability of analyses. Counters will tell you how many times your ad has been viewed, how many people clicked through, which pages they visited and how much time they spent there. You can also monitor more detailed information such as search terms used or which website viewers originally came from.

We have already mentioned, in a previous chapter, the necessity of having a good website to promote your company. However, this is not where the possibilities of online promotion end, quite the contrary. There are many methods of promotion you can use to ensure that people can easily find you on the Internet, including:

- **Search engine marketing (SEM)**

  A form of advertising where you pay for a preferential entry in various online catalogues, have sponsored links, banners and so on. A part of SEM is pay per click (PPC) advertising.

- **PPC**

  Advertising in the form of short annotations that are shown either in search results or in articles. It is one of the most effective forms of online advertising. It can be measured very precisely and adjustments can be made easily. The principle is that you pay when people actually click through your link (pay per click) and are redirected to your website, not when your ad is displayed. A different method of charging advertisers is pay per view, which is usually used for so-called display advertising using banners.

- **Promotion in search engines for free**

  If you don't like the previous options and you still want your company website to appear at the top of searches, you should hire a search engine optimization (SEO) expert who will optimize your website to make it attractive and relevant to search engines. An SEO expert can adjust your website structure and content so that search engines index – save – in their databases the maximum number of keywords used on your website. SEO experts can also work with so-called backlinks: they find website owners who will place a link to your website on theirs in exchange for you placing their link on your website. This will help you get a better position in search engines.

- **Advertising on social media**

  Advertising on social media has several undisputed advantages: it enables you to reach a large number of users and, as they publish quite a lot of information about themselves (age, sex, family status, hobbies, etc.), you can select specific target groups. You are also able to monitor how the campaign is doing via various data and then change it accordingly. Since people use social media for communication, not for watching ads, you need to adjust your advertising so that it encourages interaction in the form of comments, likes and shares.

  - On **Facebook** you can place ads (for free) on your profile where your fans can see them, add comments and share. Another option is sponsored advertising where your advertisement is only displayed to the group of people whose size and demographic parameters you preselect. A third option is to pay for static advertising on the side panel of the website. This is more expensive, but you only pay when users click through.

  - On **Twitter** you just need to write an interesting or original tweet that will attract attention to your company. Then every single tweet of yours promotes your business and your short tweets may reach a great number of so-called followers, people who have signed up to receive your tweets.

  - **YouTube** may be used in several different ways. You can either create your own marketing video – but, of course, it must be entertaining enough that people watch it. Making such a video doesn't have to be expensive and, if you decide to shoot one, you will certainly use it for presentation purposes elsewhere too, not just on social media. You can make a video manual or a short film showing your customers' reactions. Or you can also place a video ad that will be shown at the start of videos uploaded by somebody else.

Vanessa Vinos quit her job as a criminal psychologist in order to start an online jewellery boutique. While living in Spain, Vanessa found that whenever she returned to the UK her friends and family would covet the jewellery she had bought from Spanish and Italian designers. That gave her the idea for Luxuria. "In Spain, people are still not big on online shopping, so the most effective way for me to get my biz known was literally via word of mouth and networking. Here in the UK, it's been using social media platforms to get new customers." Vanessa had always wanted a business that she could run from anywhere. She wanted to be "location-independent". Therefore, a brick-and-mortar shop was out of the question. "So for me, what I love most is the freedom to plan my day and not work to someone else's timetable. Also, to be able to jump on a plane whenever I want and take my work with me. I don't care if I have to work until 2 in the morning if I am working from a lovely place." (16)
(Vanessa Vinos, UK)

Social media offers more possibilities for promotion than just advertising. You can use it on several fronts under your **SMM (social media marketing)** umbrella. This communication channel offers space for direct communication with your customers, such as holding various contests. It works as a PR tool and allows you to receive valuable feedback from your customers. Social media is beneficial for brand building and great for making special offers.

Social media works perfectly for companies that can work proactively with their fans. One-sided communication with customers is not enough. You need to prompt your fans to interact with you and establish a friendly dialogue with them. I accentuate the word "friendly" as any arrogant or inappropriate response from your side could have a lasting effect on the company reputation. Communication should be natural, relaxed, easy and, above all, continuous.

In addition to highly sophisticated and paid forms of advertising on the Internet or elsewhere, there is one more very efficient way you can spread awareness of your products. It has been proven over centuries, it is free and it is becoming popular again. It is word of mouth. According to Global Trust in Advertising 2015, a study by Nielsen (17), the number of consumers who trust so-called earned media – that is, what they learn via word of mouth, what their family or friends recommend to them – has significantly increased in recent years. One reason for this growing trend may be the arrival of so-called generation C, which is characterized by permanent connection to the Internet and a strong social nature. This generation doesn't care about brands or one-sided communication that they cannot interact with. On the contrary, they attach great importance to their peers' recommendations, rather than to any other forms of advertising.

No wonder. As has already been said, most people are tired of – almost resistant to – the continuous flood of commercials and advertising. During commercial breaks on TV we go to make a coffee or change channels. When we are in the car we switch radio stations as soon as we hear a persuasive voice offering us cheap holidays by the sea or the services of a great floor-laying company, and we try to ignore the billboards alongside the road. But when a friend of ours mentions the wonderful hand cream she uses or a new shop with lights, we prick up our ears and listen to her attentively. Even the best thought-out media campaign cannot beat a personal recommendation that goes from mouth to mouth and from ear to ear. Word of mouth is not only effective, but also cheap, which doesn't mean it is free. You "buy" it with frequent and smart activities on social media. In particular, by systematically building up your reputation with a decent and friendly approach to your customers (face to face as well as online) and honest hard work from the very beginning, not turning down any orders, even if they're small and not so lucrative for you. You never know, a small client of yours might mention a great purchase they have made from you in front of a person who later turns out to be your biggest customer.

As Godfrey and Gregory Harris write in *101 Ways to Promote Your Business* (18), the positive effect of word of mouth can be supported with the following:

- **Give out presents**
  People who get a present usually display it in a visible place and speak about the donor. And what about your customers' children when they get a small gift from you (e.g. a lolly, balloon, paper ruler)?

- **Do things differently**
  Customers usually speak highly of those who provide them with a service that is unusual or is done in a way that is particularly beneficial to them.

- **Keep your clients busy**

  Offer your clients rewards and advantages they can share with other people – this way you'll easily win other fans. If you, for instance, decide to offer a certain service to your prospective clients for free or at a discount, have this information printed on vouchers that your current customers may hand over to people they know.

- **Spread information**

  Tell your clients about something new, interesting or humorous that they could share with others. Then you'll profit if the listeners ask them: "Who did you hear that from?"

- **Minimize negative impressions**

  You cannot avoid deserved or undeserved negative reactions, but you may moderate their impact with immediate responses: by apologizing, offering a discount voucher for their next purchase and so on.

Harris and Harris (18) suggest that in order to support advertising by word of mouth, you need to make it easy for your customers to promote you. You should feed them the themes and issues that they will then bring up when talking about your company with others. Remind them what it is that you do faster, better and cheaper than your competition. Provide examples of what you have produced and who your customers were. Try this approach with the first customer you come across. If their response is positive, you've found a good argument for other customers.

There are agencies that specialize in this kind of support. You can hire them to help this "word of mouth" buzz get started a little quicker.

5. PEOPLE

Originally, there were the 4Ps in the marketing mix, but later on a fifth was added: people. People as a marketing mix tool represent added value, together with the product purchased by the end customer in the form of experience, expertise, know-how and services. Simply said, it is mainly about the service you provide. Take a look at banks, for instance. It doesn't matter how good their services and products are. Who is actually the bank to you? The clerk sitting at the desk! This person influences how happy you are and for you is the face of the financial institution. If he or she's not helpful and doesn't give you good answers to your questions, the bank will probably lose you as a customer. So, you should pick your employees and colleagues very carefully regardless of what type of business you run. Remember that the people you choose will be the face of your company!

PUBLIC RELATIONS

From word of mouth we can smoothly proceed to PR. The purpose of PR is to achieve, enhance and maintain the good reputation of your company, develop awareness of your brand, services and products, and provide information and news. To put it another way, sales support. PR activities usually look more trustworthy than advertising, as the general public doesn't tend to see them as advertisements.

Unlike advertising, PR activities are not so expensive, but their effects do not usually become evident immediately. PR tools include:

- **Publications** (e.g. company magazine, publications on company anniversaries)

- **Company events** (e.g. new product presentations, awards, parties for important clients)
- **Information materials** (e.g. press releases, articles, brochures, infographics)
- **Involvement in the local community** (e.g. investments, efforts to be engaged in community activities and events)
- **Company culture** (e.g. corporate identity across all communication – that is, from business card design to signage at the company premises, to vehicle livery and company uniforms)
- **Lobbying** (e.g. critical PR aimed at remedying negative consequences of an adverse event that could harm the company reputation)
- **Corporate social responsibility – CSR** (e.g. ecological manufacturing, adequate conditions for employees, involvement with charity)

Obviously, as is the case in other specialized fields, in PR you can buy the specialist services of an agency that will help you communicate. Such an agency regularly assesses all your PR activities and you receive weekly or monthly overviews of, for example, how many PR articles have been published about your company, in which periodicals, how many of them were taken up by other media and what the tone was: whether they were positive, negative or neutral.

What you can certainly do yourself is to keep the media informed with press releases – if you have the right contacts, this method of communication doesn't cost much but is very effective. You should expect that the message you want to tell the world will be distorted a little, since the final form of each article is usually adjusted by magazine and newspaper editors (unless it is a paid PR article), but the total gain still exceeds the potential negatives. Don't be shy to get in touch with the media and journalists. Their task is to fill blank spaces (or spaces in TV or radio broadcasting), which is not easy. They'll certainly welcome useful and clearly presented information, so why hesitate if you have something to offer?

You must be inventive with how you present the information you're offering. In other words, the question isn't just WHAT you are offering, but also HOW.

Let's say that your gardening company plans to rent Christmas trees in flowerpots over the Christmas period. There are almost an infinite number of possibilities as to how you can talk about that, such as:

1. Send out a press release with brief information about this novelty you're about to launch. It will certainly do no harm, although it is not guaranteed that you'll attract interest.
2. Send out a press release with brief information about the novelty including a list of its advantages (saving money, protecting the environment, etc.) along with survey results documenting a growing interest in this service. This will increase your chances, as journalists love exact and well-documented facts, advice and tips.
3. Order a courier and send your press release together with a small tree in a flowerpot. Again, there's a high chance that you'll strike gold, since journalists (just like all of us) love presents and they'll appreciate your inventiveness.

There's something else that works well – the inclusion of the human factor, stories and numbers. Your press release could include stories about giving trees to families that have fallen on hard times, celebrities in your region or institutions (e.g. a nursery school, children's play centre, children's home) or inform people that you're holding a contest for the most beautifully decorated tree in a flowerpot. Don't forget to put the photographs of trees you receive on your website and on social media with a couple of lines saying what the contestants found under their Christmas trees, for example. Even when doing PR activities, you still need to think about your target audience, but otherwise you can let your creativity run wild.

So, how should you write a press release that doesn't end up in the bin? Start by considering the following:

- **Would the topic you're writing about catch your interest if you were the reader?**
  Your message should be fresh, topical, interesting, useful, supported by facts and you should be able to put it in one sentence. Of course, when a company buys new software it makes paper pushing easier, but will it have any impact on the services they provide to customers? Don't flood the media with what they will see as banalities, instead focus on informing people about substantial matters and try to present them from the most interesting point of view. You should also consider whether the best format for telling the given news is a press release, or if it would actually be better to hold a press conference, contact a particular journalist or pay for a PR article.

- **Write briefly and clearly**
  A journalist must find, in each press release, answers to basic questions: who, what, when, where, how and why. All the facts must be clearly and understandably arranged; there's no place for riddles, ambiguities and unanswered questions. Use

the data you have and don't forget to put it into context. A traditional press release should always fit on a single A4 page. Remember to include the date and contact details for someone who can answer any questions. You might add a link for downloading photographs with a high, printable resolution.

- **Forget about self-praise**
  The structure of a press release should be simple and well arranged. Put the most important message in the first sentence, then you can expand on it with less important details and context. You should also state at the beginning what significance or impact the news may have on the general public. Never keep important information or any other potentially surprising message for the end. It could easily happen that a journalist doesn't read that far. Write briefly and clearly in short paragraphs and sentences. You're writing for laypeople, so you should avoid expert terms. Forget about self-praise and superlatives that are not supported by facts. Use at least two endorsements in your press release, preferably from two different people.

- **A moderate style demonstrates your seriousness**
  Creativity is undesirable in a formal press release. You should choose a moderate approach and traditional style. Use your logo in the heading, write the text in a traditional font (e.g. Times New Roman, Arial, Tahoma), and quotations may be in italics. Save press releases in .doc or .pdf formats that can be opened on any computer.

- **Be accommodating, but don't exert pressure**
  Contact media that your target market read, follow or listen to.

Naturally, you can send a message to a national paper saying that you're opening a new beauty salon in Plymouth, but the likelihood of this news being published is zero. Don't send the press release to everyone. Select your recipients carefully, otherwise you'll get the reputation of a spammer. Don't be lazy. Look for journalists who write about the field in which you run your business, or send an email to an editor who has the contents of each issue recorded. There is high fluctuation in the media, so you should keep your media list updated. With respect to the scope of your activities, you may need to get several media lists.

Send your press releases on working days, not at the weekends or on Fridays, and preferably in the morning so that the journalist or editor in question can include it in the upcoming issue or broadcast. If your press release is about a particular event, it should be sent on the day when it takes place.

Be open and communicative when talking to journalists. Offer your "goods", but don't impose yourself relentlessly. Newspapers are sensitive to external pressure. No matter how much you care if a journalist has used or intends to use your press release, call each of them just once. It is especially important to prepare for a possible increase of interest in your goods and services – after all, growth is the main purpose of PR activities.

There are situations when it is more effective to hold a press conference. However, you should consider this very carefully, as holding a press conference is more expensive than a press release. Again, look at it from the outside – while every advancement in the business is important to you, uninterested people probably won't care about it. Moreover, journalists are very busy, so they carefully pick the events they attend in person and they compare the invested time with gain. (Nevertheless, it may still happen that they won't attend your press conference for some reason, but they'll ask you to send them your press materials, which is almost a victory for you.)

Entering the market, developing an important new product, introducing a break-through or interesting service, dismissing employees, economic results, activities concerning social responsibility and so on – these are all events that justify a press conference. By contrast, when you're appointing a new sales manager, introducing new packaging or changing the headquarters, for example, it is enough to inform the media by sending a press release (if anything at all).

When sending invitations to your press conference, use the contacts from your media list. Don't phone journalists. They're most likely to tell you to send them the information by email anyway. Make sure the invitation contains details such as the place, date and time, including the programme with names of the speakers. If it is not clear how to get to the place where the event is held (company headquarters, lounge in a restaurant or hotel, etc.) enclose directions or at least a link to a map. Provide some refreshment (e.g. mineral water, coffee, tea), technical equipment (portable microphone, devices for PowerPoint presentations, etc.) and have somebody welcoming guests at the door and collecting their business cards.

The essential thing, of course, is to have good press materials ready – it is customary that upon arrival participants find all the information they're going to hear in a folder (written on headed paper with your business card attached), on a CD or on a flash drive. They may not then be motivated to listen to every word they're going to hear, but the advantage is that you know they have all the information from you. You should certainly allow some time for questions at the end. Upon leaving, some press conference holders give journalists a small present, but choose it rather carefully as it should not look like a bribe. On the other hand, it should not be a souvenir "left over" from a previous event – a calendar for a year that is about to end or a clearly obsolete guidebook, for example. Naturally, the ideal present somehow relates to the topic of your press conference.

QUESTIONS TO CONSIDER

DO I HAVE A MARKETING STRATEGY AND MARKETING PLAN?
The sooner you start gathering background materials, the better.

IF NOT, DO YOU HAVE AN IDEA WHICH MARKETING MIX TOOLS WOULD COME IN HANDY FOR A START-UP?
Draw on who your target market is.

DO I KNOW HOW MUCH I WANT OR CAN AFFORD TO INVEST IN MARKETING ACTIVITIES?
Investment in marketing shouldn't be underestimated, even in times of crisis.

WHAT PROMOTIONAL FORMATS WILL HELP ME ADVERTISE MY BUSINESS MOST EFFECTIVELY?
Focus especially on the Internet and social media.

IF I DO PR ACTIVITIES MYSELF, DO I HAVE ENOUGH CONTACTS TO COMPILE A MEDIA LIST (JOURNALISTS WHO WRITE ABOUT MY FIELD OF BUSINESS)? DO I KNOW HOW I AM GOING TO INFORM THE PUBLIC ABOUT WHAT'S GOING ON IN MY COMPANY? CAN I WRITE A PRESS RELEASE?
Try to have a dry run at writing a press release and ask someone who doesn't know anything about the given topic to critique it.

Chapter 12

Cast your nets wide

If you're not on the Internet, you don't exist

It doesn't matter what industry you're starting up your business in, what matters is that you let the world know that you're there! It is vital for each company to be visibly present online, as that is now the primary source of information for the majority of people. Everyone is online these days, wherever they are, and – thanks to the Internet on mobile phones – almost nonstop. How can this be used to the advantage of your business?

YOU CAN REACH A MUCH BIGGER GROUP OF POTENTIAL CUSTOMERS

Not only in the country where you want to run your business, but internationally. What if your local business suddenly expands abroad simply because you win a customer somewhere you didn't expect? Have an open mind and make use of all the advantages the Internet brings. It is the most flexible communication channel and it allows you to start doing your marketing right now. It is also the most effective channel, as you can target precisely and assess information easily, so you know immediately what works and what doesn't.

THE INTERNET IS USED PRIMARILY TO SEARCH FOR INFORMATION

If people find you on the Internet, learn more about you and you catch their interest, you've increased your chances of selling your products or services.

IF YOU'RE ON THE INTERNET, YOU'RE AVAILABLE 24/7

This is very important these days. Look at it from your own perspective. Do you want to buy a cake for your kids? Thanks to the Internet you can search for a suitable cake shop at 7 am or at midnight. Thanks to online enquiry and order forms used by most companies on their websites, you can contact a baker at any time.

THE INTERNET PROVIDES A WIDE RANGE OF WAYS TO PUT YOURSELF ON THE MAP

By doing this, you will simultaneously be supporting your business through search engines and social networks.

THE INTERNET, ESPECIALLY SOCIAL MEDIA, ENABLES BETTER COMMUNICATION WITH CUSTOMERS

This will also help you when building relationships with customers. In particular, thanks to the Internet, you can receive feedback from your clients and encourage two-way communication. Whether it is positive or negative, it is crucial for every business. It is direct, meaning that it is not mediated by anyone else, and honest, simply stated: it is the most valuable feedback.

INTERNET ACTIVITY ASSESSMENT TOOLS PROVIDE VALUABLE STATISTICS

You'll obtain very detailed information about the people who search for you on the Internet. You'll know how many of them there are (business potential), if their interest in your products or services grows or falls, where these people are located (locally, abroad, whether they use the Internet at home or on portable devices) and how much time they spent on your website and on what pages. All of this will help you plan further steps for growth and improve your current activities.

THE CURTAIN FELL ON THE YELLOW PAGES LONG AGO, PEOPLE ARE USED TO SEARCHING FOR EVERYTHING ON THE INTERNET

When searching for a specific company or product, if nothing else, people use the Internet at least to find the address of the nearest brick-and-mortar shop. So, if you want people to find you, you must be online, whatever you do and whatever you offer. What does that mean for you? First of all, you need a professional, well-arranged and attractive company website. But there's so much more the Internet has to offer...

A STEPPING STONE FOR SUCCESS

The first thing each company should invest in is a good website that should be ready to launch before you actually start your business. The website is also important from the perspective of search engines that evaluate the quality of websites to determine their rank in search results. Your goal should be to achieve a top position in the search results. How can you do that? You have two options: either you create your website yourself or you hire a professional.

Making a company website that both has an attractive design and is optimized for search engines is not an easy task. If you can afford it, you should definitely hire somebody, whether it is a web designer or a company that specializes in bespoke website design. You might opt for anything from a simple website to a highly sophisticated one with interactive features. In the latter case, you should expect to pay thousands of pounds. However, this investment will provide a return in the form of new clients and opportunities. This is what it is all about, right? If you decide to hire such a company, you should follow your friends' recommendations, look at references (portfolio of websites created), ask how successful their previously designed websites are. If you're considering making the website yourself, you'll probably want to use a template. There are many of them on the Internet and they will save you a great deal of time and effort.

Small and medium-sized businesses may prefer to employ freelancers, who can also make custom websites. Usually freelancers offer more favourable prices, as everything is done by a single person, rather than an army of specialists such as a graphic designer, programmer, copywriter and SEO specialist. However, choosing a freelancer doesn't mean that the web design he or she creates won't meet your needs, especially if such a person is a real professional. (For instance, in the UK the UKWDA is a good place to start looking at profiles of web-design freelancers www.ukwda.org, as well as www.odesk.com).

THINK OF YOUR VISITORS

In a previous chapter, you did an analysis of your target market; the same analysis is also important when you're creating your company website. Who will it be for? Who are your potential customers? You need to know whether these will be predominantly women or men, what their socio-demographic profile is (age, sex, education, income, interests, habits, etc.) and what their needs are. All of this should be reflected in your website. A website aimed at students will certainly look very different from one directed at retired people.

You also should define what your expectations are. What purpose will your website serve? Is it intended to be primarily informative, or should it be a detailed guide to the products or services you offer? It can also be a selling channel or a means of communication with your clients, or it can meet all of these requirements.

If you're running a little shop in a small town, a simple website where your customers can find your address and contact details, including your phone number, information about your opening hours, plus maybe some news, will be perfectly adequate. However, it is a completely different story if you intend to run an e-shop selling sports equipment, for example, where the website is the primary location for presenting your business and products, and what generates your profit. Then the presence of your website online is obviously crucial. There are countless variants between these two extreme examples. Now take a pencil and paper and try to describe your situation.

Here is one more example: what online representation do you need if you're running a family hotel? Your customers will be primarily tourists and visitors from other regions, such as businesspeople, so they'll be searching for you on the Internet. Your website should entice them to visit your hotel and should thus contain at the very least an inquiry form, accommodation pricelists, a photo gallery and contact details.

"I'm glad I'm living in the times of the Internet. If I had wanted to sell goods some years ago, I would have had to open a brick-and-mortar shop, but today there's nothing easier than having an e-shop. And that's exactly what I want to do. Being a programmer, it shouldn't be a problem for me. My maternity leave is about to end, and I'm one of those mothers who decided to take advantage of their break from work and change their profession. After my son was born, a new world opened up to me and I found, among other things, how many high-quality products and great gadgets there are that facilitate parents tak-

ing care of their babies. An e-shop is the perfect solution for me because I can work while still looking after my little son. Moreover, my clients socialize on my website. Mothers of small babies love the Internet."

(Linda, 28, Belgium)

BEING YOUR OWN WEB DESIGNER

If you've decided to design your website yourself, the following steps will take you through the basic process and should make the task a lot easier.

DOMAIN NAME AND HOSTING

First you need to choose a suitable domain name, which is your website address.

Look at it through the eyes of your customers. What keywords would you use to search for what it is you're offering? Use your common sense and choose an address that is simple, fitting and easy to remember. First you should check if this domain name (or a very similar one) has already been taken. You can also check what domain names your competitors use.

Don't forget about the extension: in addition to .uk you may use .ie, .org, .com or .eu. Before you can get your website online, you need to choose a hosting provider.

CONTENT MANAGEMENT SYSTEM

Now you need to select your content management system. This determines the basics and restrictions of your website. At the same time, it influences whether or not your website will be a static company presentation or will include an e-shop or other useful features. The less complicated this system is, the less work you'll have with your website administration.

The quickest way to get your website up and running is to design it online. You don't need any special knowledge or software. All you need is a browser, and you can have your website ready in a couple of minutes. You can administer it via an online interface, you don't need to worry about the technical background as this is handled by the service provider.

Don't give in to luring offers of generating your website for free. These platforms are very basic and generally suitable only for personal websites. It pays to invest in the online presentation of your company. For that matter, why not compare the free and paid platforms for options.

You can make simple websites via a number of platforms. One of the most frequently used open source content management systems, in many countries, is **WordPress** (www.wordpress.com). You can easily design your own website with the templates provided, even if you don't have any real knowledge of programming. You are the one who decides on the appearance and functionality with the numerous graphic templates and plug-ins (accessory software extending the functionality). Other well-known open source content management systems, besides WordPress, are **Drupal** and **Joomla!**

Now that you know what your options are, you need to look around and choose the best solution for you. If you aren't very well versed in this field, pick one of the options offered for beginners.

ATTRACTIVE PACKAGING IS NOT ENOUGH

Even the most attractive website will not bring you success if you don't fill it with good content. Website content goes hand in hand with SEO, which we mentioned in the previous chapter about marketing. The content of your website must be schematic, understandable and regularly updated – not only for your customers, but also for search engines that assess websites' attractiveness with respect to their content. Where your website is positioned in search results depends on whether it is correctly structured, contains the right number of appropriate keywords, uses correctly described images and has relevant headings for each page.

One thing is for sure: if the "robots" don't find your content interesting, clients will never see your site. Therefore, we can say that SEO plays a major part in making a company successful on the Internet. What are the implications for you? The better the content, the better the search results. After all, you know from your own experience that people generally only look at the first five or six search results on the first page and don't bother to scroll down any further.

When writing pieces of text for your website, you should think not only of your potential customer, but also of search engines. In particular:

- Use keywords the search engines will index.
- Don't overdo it with keywords, otherwise the search engines will penalize you and you won't appear among top search results.
- Keep in mind that useful, informative and well written content is essential for succeeding in search engines, as they will easily pick up on low-quality or unoriginal content and many companies (websites) have been penalized for this.

WHAT ARE KEYWORDS?

Internet search engines use information from your website and present search results accordingly. One of the criteria for assessing whether your website is highly relevant to a particular search is keywords. A keyword is a word (or phrase) that describes most accurately your product or service. Keywords are what people type into their search engines. If the content is optimized, search engines will display those sites to the viewer as soon as they evaluate it as being relevant to the keywords entered.

Once you have come up with the keywords that best describe your business activities, get down to writing the text for your website and try to use these words –not only in the text, but also in the headings, descriptions of photographs and meta description. The general rule is to use one keyword per one hundred words of text.

If writing is not your strong point, you can hire a professional copywriter who will write attractive content for you.

CAST YOUR SOCIAL NETS

Social media is becoming more and more important in online communication and it can certainly help you strengthen the position of your company. It can be effectively used as a PR communication tool and for building your relationship with your customers. In comparison with traditional media, such as advertising in the press, on billboards or even via TV advertisements, it is much cheaper and much more effective. You only need to know how to use it to the advantage of your business.

FACEBOOK

One of the most popular social networks is, of course, Facebook (FB). It has been out there for more than a decade and, according to the statistics portal Statista, as of the second quarter of 2016 had 1.71 billion monthly active users. In the UK alone there are reportedly approximately 30 million Facebook users – a figure that is expected to grow to 33 million in 2018 (www.statista.com/statistics/271349/facebook-users-in-the-united-kingdom-uk/). Even if you don't have a personal profile, you should definitely create one for your company. Facebook doesn't cost anything and you would be throwing away a valuable opportunity to reach millions of active users with whom you can communicate every day in order to offer them your services in an attractive and unforced way. What is more, you can create advertisements on Facebook to promote your website, which you only pay for if somebody clicks through to your website.

TWITTER

Another highly popular social network, Twitter, can provide great support for your business, especially if you intend to expand globally. There are approximately 313 million monthly Twitter users around the world (19). Its uniqueness lies in the structure: writing short entries and sending pictures and links. Alongside organizations, many celebrities, actors, singers, sportspeople, fashion designers, models and TV personalities use Twitter to communicate with their fans. The content on Twitter changes with the speed of light, but thanks to the hashtag (#) functions and retweeting it is ideal for getting information about companies. You can use Twitter to communicate with people directly in order to present your company to them personally and informally.

INSTAGRAM

Companies often neglect this application, although sharing photographs may be just as useful as sharing texts, especially when there are 500 million users worldwide each month [20]. You can share photographs of goods or services, especially if you're running your business in the field of lifestyle (e.g. food, fashion, luxury brands) where the visual aspect supports sales more than it does in some other fields. You can also utilize celebrities for the promotion of your brand. This doesn't need to look like advertising and has been shown to skyrocket sales. A staggering 48.8 per cent of brands are on Instagram. By 2017, this is predicted to rise to 70.7 per cent.

This trend can be observed especially in the clothing industry, where it is often thanks to celebrities who show a new piece of their clothing on Instagram that a particular item is sold out in a couple of hours. If we only look at the top hundred brands in the world, 90 per cent have an Instagram account, and that rises to 96 per cent for US fashion brands.

Engagement with brands on Instagram is ten times higher than Facebook, fifty-four times higher than Pinterest and eighty-four times higher than Twitter [19]. You need to approach this with some thought.

PINTEREST

Pinterest is a social medium with 100 million monthly users globally [19] where people can create "notice boards" onto which they can "pin" anything they like. One interesting entry can then be shared by hundreds or even thousands of other users. If you have your own profile here, you can publish a variety of interesting things concerning your business in relevant categories.

LINKEDIN

This is a business oriented networking platform where professionals meet – whether they are peers, HR professionals, employees, bosses or companies – to discuss their business interests. According to the global web index, four in ten Internet users are LinkedIn members (21). LinkedIn enables you to get in touch with your colleagues, even former ones, and people from other companies who can support your business. You'll also find company profiles, job offers and various expert articles.

GOOGLE+

Although there are officially 500 million users, it is thought that 90 per cent of Google accounts have never actually made a public post on Google+. Google themselves describe this as "'a social layer across all of Google's services' rather than a social network" (22). Despite not being as successful as Facebook or Twitter, you shouldn't completely ignore it. Even if you don't use it for posting entries or interaction with your customers, you should know that a company profile on Google+ is displayed in Google search engine results, which means further publicity for your business.

YOUTUBE

When you hear YouTube, a site where you can upload any video, you probably immediately think of cute videos with frolicking animals or funny goofs. However, YouTube can also be used to promote your business, and it does a great service in brand building. You can share a variety of content, including:
- Video blogs
- Product descriptions
- Video manuals
- Customer reactions and reviews

Thanks to its partner programme, you can even earn a little bit of money on YouTube. Producers of videos that are so popular they become viral earn thousands of pounds from companies who pay to run adverts in connection with the videos, in some cases even hundreds of thousands. What is more, you only pay for videos that are watched for over twenty seconds, not if viewing is interrupted before that. This can help to build awareness of your brand or product.

Of course, you don't need to use every single social networking site out there, but pick two or three that will provide the greatest contribution to your business. Maybe Instagram and Pinterest aren't necessary for you, but your business can definitely be promoted via Facebook or Twitter, maybe even LinkedIn or YouTube. All you need to do is compare what options you have and present your company professionally on the suitable sites.

"I work as an editor for a magazine and I'm interested in fashion. I decided to combine these two passions of mine in a blog, which I've been writing for two years now. I'm glad that other people are interested in my opinions and I'm pleased when I see how the numbers of visitors keep rising. I'm seriously flirting with the idea of writing blogs for a living, meaning professionally, so it doesn't have to be necessarily only about fashion. There are so many companies in the world who have a blog tab on their website, but nobody takes much care of it, although it is a great way to increase the audience of your website."

(Rachel, 25, UK)

FIND THE BLOGGER INSIDE YOURSELF

Now we've come to blogging. You may think: Oh no, that requires writing articles and writing them often! The truth is, it doesn't sound like the greatest fun in the world, unless you're an enthusiastic writer. But blogging is very important for business.

According to Nicole Beachum, the founder and managing partner of Epic Consulting, if your company doesn't have a blog where it regularly updates its content, you're missing out on a great opportunity to raise awareness of your company by expanding your digital reach and thus your potential client base and profits. In a contemporary society that is based on the Internet, organizations must have a strong online presence in order to beat the competition. When people search for an expert or company in your field, your name must be among the top search results. How can you achieve this? By having effective search engine optimization. (23)

We have already mentioned the importance of SEO in connection with website presentation, and now it should be emphasized that you can also optimize your blog content and thus attract even more attention. If you're using any of the above-mentioned tools for web design, they also offer facilities for setting up a blog. Naturally, you can also use other options such as blogger.com or Tumblr (www.tumblr.com).

A blog is another platform through which you can communicate proactively with your customers and anyone interested in your goods or services. It offers you a place to present the advantages of your offerings and respond to any questions and queries.

You may be put off writing your own blog by doubts about whether you'll have enough material or ideas to write about. For your inspiration, here's a list of several themes. When you think about them, you'll certainly come up with several specific subjects.

- How to do it (how to use the product I'm offering...)
- News (the latest product model is to appear on the market in a month...)
- Product description (this is a product and it works this way...)
- Customer reactions (what your customers said about a product...)
- Interesting stories – this is what happened to one of the co-owners yesterday (stories that somehow relate to your company can perfectly attract attention)

Once you've chosen subjects to write about and have had your first go at the writing itself, you'll certainly get the hang of blogging and writing regular entries will stop being a problem. If not, there's no point in trying too hard (readers would sense your reluctance to write in the words anyway). Instead you should do the same that applies to web design – hire a professional who'll blog for you.

When writing blog entries, remember to use keywords the same way you do when creating content for your website. As before, aim to use one keyword per hundred words of text.

PROACTIVELY BUILD YOUR COMPANY REPUTATION ON THE INTERNET

If you really want to strengthen your position, take advantage of the possibilities the Internet offers and establish yourself as an expert in your field. Don't hesitate to use the other options available to easily promote what you're doing. Write for other blogs, other companies or experts. This way you'll open doors to the public. (For that matter, you can offer this service reciprocally to the given company, as long as it is not your direct competitor). Also write articles for other relevant websites or publications.

Write informative and interesting texts from which readers will learn something new. Even if you don't promote your company directly in these materials, or there's not a link to your website next to your name, if the article is interesting, people will be willing to search for you: naturally, on the Internet. You see, we got back to how important a good Internet presence is. Now do you believe me that it is necessary for your business to succeed?

QUESTIONS TO CONSIDER

WHAT SHOULD MY WEBSITE LOOK LIKE?

You need to know who you want to address with your website and adjust its design, structure and content accordingly. You also need to decide if you're going to entrust professionals with the web design or if you're going to do it yourself.

WHICH SOCIAL MEDIA PLATFORMS ARE BEST FOR ME?

Opening an account won't take you long. Pick at least two networks and try them out. Except for time, it won't cost you anything.

DO I HAVE ENOUGH IDEAS FOR BLOG ENTRIES?

Look once again at the general themes presented in this chapter and think of at least five topics.

Chapter 13

How did you do it, granny?

How to build a company that will outlive you

It is only natural that when you're starting up your business you must focus primarily on the present moment so that things work here and now. At the same time, you need to think about what the steps you're taking today will mean in the future. This is easier said than done, especially when you are new to business. You may not be able to tell the difference between a company that will shine bright yet burn out like a comet and a company that will easily outlive you.

The US magazine Entrepreneur published an article on this topic (24) which analyses three different companies with more than a hundred years of tradition: Nelson Trucking (on the market since 1901), Manson Construction (since 1905) and Mutual Materials (since 1900). The article tries to answer the question of how their owners managed to build companies that have been successful over the long term. The most important principles that owners of successful companies adhere to include:

- They always focus on their core business and don't succumb to the temptation to accommodate everyone.
- They make sure their company keeps developing and adjust their products to contemporary requirements. Mutual Materials, for example, made popular thin "Roman" bricks in the 1940s and 1950s. Today, the same company is making products out of stone. Why? Because it is currently the most popular material.

- They rarely struggle with fluctuations; a large percentage of their employees stay long term and some are "lifelong" employees who have become the trustworthy "brains" of the company. Moreover, the continuity of owners has reached the third generation.
- They prioritize taking care of their employees. Although profit is primary, the management of these companies take good care of their employees, provide them with employment benefits and in some cases even pay salaries as requested by trade unions.
- They always search for opportunities to grow. For instance, Manson has 700 employees now with branches in California, Florida and Louisiana. The latter helped fix the devastation left behind by hurricane Katrina. The company ensures that it is where the big projects are being implemented.

All three of these companies are good examples of what should be done and what should be avoided if you want to be successful in the long term. It doesn't matter that you're going to be in a completely different industry, these practices are universally applicable. It doesn't matter if you run a shop selling lights or a pastry shop.

How should you set up your business so that your company is successful for many years to come? Let's divide the tips and recommendations into several categories: resources, employees, marketing and your general view of your business.

The First World War was anything but a business opportunity, yet Coco Chanel saw her chance during this period. Women needed functional working clothes and she tried to comply with their requirements. Coco Chanel's style was born. The fashion designer who influenced the style of the century and changed the lives of so many women was an unconventional person. She claimed to be an anarchist and the antithesis of everything. And she actually behaved that way. She worked hard on both her career and her image. The last years of her life were spent covering her tracks, fudging information about her private life and disowning her parents, siblings and lovers. She totally denied her losses, personal as well as business ones. She used to say that we must all handle our mistakes: who learns to use them to their benefit, gains everything. (25)

ECONOMIZE, BUT ONLY IN THE RIGHT PLACES

One of the most common reasons a new company gets in trouble is that it uses up all the available resources too fast. These may include human resources, materials, information, technology, energy and time. Unreasonable management at the very beginning, however well intended, in an effort to make everything work right from the start, may place you in dire straits and, in some cases, you may have no other option but to "shut up shop". It is similar to when you pack some food for a day trip, but you eat everything on the way there.

TWO-PART PLAN

You need to anticipate that every new company may face hard times that need to be overcome as soon as possible. If you always want to have enough resources, you have two options:

- Try using resources to gain the longest term benefit. If you get a loan, consider how you're going to use the money. Is buying new furniture for your meeting room really a priority at the moment?
- Add new resources gradually and sensibly as your business develops. After you start earning money, what will you do with the profit? Will you pay the bills and use the rest to pay for your child's private school tuition? Or will you invest the money back into your company so that money makes more money?

The right approach is to do both at the same time. The exact description of how to handle your resources sensibly at every stage should always be defined in your business plan.

CHOOSE THE RIGHT GOALS

Getting your business going may be expensive. You will be forced to spend money on many things, and the way in which you handle money will influence how long your resources will last. What can't you save on when trying to achieve the best business results possible?

As has already been said several times, marketing is crucial for business and as soon as you have the products or services you intend to offer ready, get down to promoting your brand. Without a conscientiously designed marketing plan, you'll be unlikely to reach the point where you start generating profit. And that is something you cannot afford when you start a business. It would be like opening a parents' centre and then spending the first two months arranging toys in cupboards, adjusting your coffee machine and sweeping the floor without letting mothers and fathers of small children in your town know about the existence of your centre. How much do you think you would earn in these two months? Certainly very little (only from passers-by perhaps), but you would spend a lot (rent, utilities, loan payments, salary for your receptionist, etc.).

"In today's world, every business is open, and everyone has the potential to market your product for you, or slate it. So when creating and implementing your marketing plan, it is important to think about your branding and how you want your business to be perceived, both in the short and longer term", writes James Caan in his article in The Guardian. He gives an example of two students who started a new company and got a loan for the development of their mobile application JumpIn. This application enables users to book and share taxi rides and tries to destroy the belief that travelling this way is dangerous – which is achieved by offering services to a trusted group of people. "Ryan and Williams are students at Leeds University, so the obvious demographic to initially roll out JumpIn to was fellow students, with a long-term plan to expand the concept to other safe, specified consumer groups. When devising their marketing strategy, the pair's three key aims were brand awareness, generating downloads and encouraging use. Brand perception was paramount when targeting these areas through various marketing channels", writes Caan (26).

As we can see, both students planned for many future years, so they were able to use their resources (that is the loan money) accordingly. In order to do the same, answer the following questions:

- Who do I need to focus on when promoting my new company, product or service?
- How do I want people to perceive my company, product or service today and in the future?
- What part of my resources can I afford to invest in marketing?

INVEST WISELY AND KEEP EARNING MORE

Once you've set up a company and invested all your money in the development of your product or improving your service, how will your customers find you? They won't! It will end similarly to the above-mentioned day care centre that you've equipped beautifully with toys, furniture and a powerful coffee machine, but have failed to promote. If customers don't know you exist, or misunderstand what you're doing, it will significantly impact the growth and success of your business.

You mustn't approach your resources too generously, don't spend them all at once. But you shouldn't be too conservative either, don't economize in the wrong places. Of course, you must invest a certain amount of your resources in the development of your product or service at the start of your business, but you should invest the majority of the available resources in:

- Branding – that is, building the right image of your company.
- Marketing and advertising – that is, publishing and spreading information about the existence of your company.

After some time, when your brand is imprinted on people's consciousness so that they automatically recognize it, you can shift a larger amount of resources from investment in branding to marketing and focus more on your promotion.

In 1947, Estée and Joseph Lauder introduced four complexion care products to the Saks department store. Estée Lauder, an ingenious entrepreneur, owed her success to always being present in her brand's various branches until the end of her life. At the same time, she had a revolutionary approach to sales which has become the norm today. She also introduced the inclusion of product samples inside the packaging. Estée Lauder was the first cosmetic brand to have its campaigns endorsed by models and famous people. Her sons Leonard and Roland, and now also four out of her six grandchildren, have continued with this pioneer-like approach to business. They still focus on detailed research into complexion rejuvenation during sleep and the results are reflected in the millions of creams sold worldwide. Today, this cosmetic giant has twenty-eight other brands under its wing including Clinique, MAC and Bobbi Brown. (27)

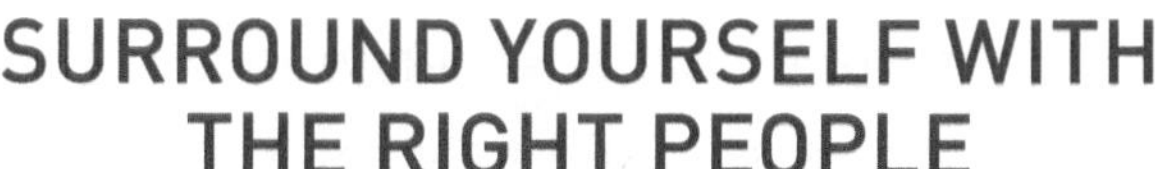

SURROUND YOURSELF WITH THE RIGHT PEOPLE

As for the long-term prosperity of your company, it is crucial to choose the right employees and create a good team. If you don't have any employees yet, you will most likely hire some sooner or later.

At the beginning of this chapter when we spoke about the business experience of long-standing companies, we spoke about the prudent selection of employees, many of whom are faithful to "their" company for many decades (and the company is faithful to them). Alan Hall (28) has outlined the optimum plan for employee recruitment, and he recommends considering the following aspects.

QUALIFICATIONS

It is logical that you want to employ people who can really do the job you hired them for. So you should ask the following:

- Does this person have the necessary qualifications to work in this position?
- Does this person have enough experience to work in this role?
- Does the person have the necessary skills for this job?

CAPABILITIES

According to Hall, capabilities differ from qualifications in that they express growth potential and willingness to take over responsibility. They have a cardinal influence on whether an employee will be able to stay in the company and develop with it.

- Will the employee be capable of completing the tasks I require from him or her?
- Will the employee be able to work independently and complete more complex tasks?
- Will the employee grow together with the company and, if necessary, work harder and assume more responsibility?

COMPATIBILITY

This relates to how an employee will integrate into the team and share its values, including ethical ones. If an employee doesn't share the company's values, there's a risk that this will be reflected in services to customers and such an employee won't fit in.

- Will this employee get on well with me and other employees?
- Can this employee tune in to the target customer group?
- If I employ this person, will it disrupt the company feel or harmony?

LOYALTY

Loyalty is irrelevant if you're looking for a part-time employee for a summer job, but if you're hiring someone for an indefinite period of time, it is absolutely crucial. A good way to find out about applicants' attitudes is to look carefully at their CVs. If somebody hasn't been in any job for more than six months or a year, ask them why they keep changing employers so often.

- Is the applicant seriously considering working for my company?
- Is the applicant interested in the job I offer as a part-time job or as full-time employment?
- How big is the risk that this applicant will leave at the first opportunity?
- Is the applicant actually interested in a different job or better conditions?

CHARACTER

Capabilities and experience are important, but character traits are sometimes even more important, as they can totally overshadow professional qualities. If you hire a lazy person whose biggest concern is how they can pass work over to a colleague, there will be no use for his or her IQ of 160. You need to realize that employee conduct will have a direct impact on your company's reputation. So check whether applicants have the same professional values as you, otherwise you risk fracturing your team, and in extreme situations even losing customers. Check the references of every candidate.

- What are the applicant's work values?
- Does this person look trustworthy? Is the person reliable? Do they keep their word?

- Does the applicant seem like a team player and an honest person who cares about a nice atmosphere and the company's prosperity?

COMPANY CULTURE

Naturally, we're not talking about how the applicant was raised or about his or her private life – after all, that's none of your business. We're talking about business culture, linked to your principles and processes, work values and expectations. All your employees have accepted this culture and respect it, and it is important that every new employee is capable of the same, otherwise, they won't fit in with the team.

REMUNERATION

Consider what salary and other bonuses you can offer to the applicant. Your offer should reflect the current situation on the labour market and the applicant should express full satisfaction with such an offer, otherwise they might start working for you with a feeling of injustice believing they deserve more. Adequate remuneration for work will help you keep good and loyal employees who will become the mainstay of your company.

PLANS ARE MADE TO BE CHANGED

This was mentioned in the chapter dedicated to designing your business plan, but there is no harm in stressing it again: A business plan is not a document set in stone. If there is anything that is sure in life, and in business, it is change. Imagine you're running an electronics business. Just because you started your business when the biggest thing on the market was the tape recorder, would you still give this preference and ignore the popularity of other devices and digital music? Try to guess how long you would survive with such a strategy. Probably not very long, because companies need to be continually evolving and responding to ever-changing customer needs.

How can you make sure that your company doesn't lag behind, but keeps developing? Try to see your business plan as a map where you see your way from point A to point B. As the landscape changes, so does your map, and your journey from A to B takes a different route. Similarly, in business you need to react to changes in the world around you, so the most successful business plans are those that are flexible.

Don't ponder too long what the distant future holds, but focus on changes you can anticipate or that are just on the horizon. Be ready to reassess your current business and marketing plan at any time, since the way you're addressing your customers today may stop working tomorrow, in a month, in a year... Get ready for it:

- Concentrate on your own business, but keep an eye on what your competition are doing.
- Evaluate your marketing regularly to see which methods led to the desired effect and which didn't meet your expectations.
- Watch for developments in marketing, especially the quickly changing marketing methods in social media and on the Internet in general. Keep pace with them.
- Find out your customers' preferences. Be interested in their reactions, results of customer behaviour surveys and so on. Update your marketing plan accordingly.

OFFERING SOMETHING NEW? BE RATHER MODERATE

People crave innovation, but at the same time refuse changes that are way too radical. Imagine if you went to McDonald's and found curry or pizza on the menu. You must always strike the right balance between your customers' expectations and something that will update what your company offers in a desirable way.

First of all, you need to find out what your customers like and what they come to you for. Once you know this, think how you could vary or extend your offer. Certainly don't change everything when innovating, you'd only confuse your customers and maybe even lose some of them. Look at McDonald's: they are and always will be a fast food chain selling hamburgers. However, this doesn't prevent its management from coming up with new ideas for diversifying their offer (e.g. new sauces, extras). You need to find the right level of innovation without going to extremes.

If you've been offering the same goods for many years, your customers may start to see your brand as boring and out of style. If you overdo it and leave no stone unturned, you'll make your clients angry and put them off. Innovate with consideration.

QUESTIONS TO CONSIDER

AM I CLEAR ABOUT THE RESOURCES AVAILABLE AND HOW THEY CAN BE USED AT THE START OF MY BUSINESS?

Think through how you're going to use the resources you have available so that you don't spend everything too soon.

WHAT ARE THE QUALITIES YOU REQUIRE IN A GOOD EMPLOYEE?

Be clear about what makes an employee highly valuable.

Chapter 14

Burning the candle at both ends, without burning out

Eleven tips for running a business marathon without collapsing

Are you busy starting up your business and looking forward to having a rest later on. But when will this "later on" be? In a month, half a year, a year or two? The bad news is that such a time probably won't magically arrive. Doing business is for the long haul, and once you cast off, you must keep rowing, maintaining the necessary tempo and direction in order to avoid all the obstacles in your way and ensure your boat doesn't become a wreck after you take the first hit. The good news is that the decision about if and when you're going to take time off is in your hands. If you want to stay healthy and have a successful business over the long term, reserve for yourself regular relaxation times. It is one of the recommendations I'd like to make at the end of this book.

You've probably already heard or read about most of what I'm going to say in this chapter. I will take the liberty of repeating some information anyway, as it is important that at least some of it gets into your blood. Not only is it important that you're aware of these points, you should also adopt them and live by them.

1. TAKE CUSTOMER SERVICE SERIOUSLY

That's only natural, I hear you say. But still, there are many entrepreneurs who primarily care about their profit: "What's in it for me?" It is not a contradiction and it is absolutely fine for people to think of themselves and their needs. However, thoughts of personal profit should only be a part of your thoughts on the subject of how you can best satisfy your customers' needs. In other words, if you satisfy your customers' needs, you'll profit from it, but it doesn't work the other way around.

That's why it is true that "the customer is always right". Of course, you mustn't apply this literally. The lady who bought chocolates from you and now wants her money back because her grandson has a stomach ache isn't necessarily right. What I mean is that it is much better to settle the matter with her in a friendly way instead of arguing. You need to bear in mind that your customers are the energy of your business. Don't ask what your company can do for you, ask what it can do for your customers.

2. LEARN THE DIFFERENCE BETWEEN A GOOD AND BAD SELLER

Have you ever negotiated with a real estate agent, financial consultant or insurance broker? Most of these professions are notoriously famed for their vigour and persistence – they want you to agree to the deal before you have had a chance to think their offer through. They behave in such a manner partly because it is in their nature, but also because they've been thoroughly trained in the most effective selling tactics.

Their pressurizing, persuasive strategy obviously works with many people, otherwise they wouldn't be doing it. These companies are focused on quick profit, while we're talking about long-term profit here. Most people have an unpleasant aftertaste after meeting these "agents blowing hot air" and their suave rhetoric rings in your ears long afterwards. After all, one of the motivations for people to sign a contract under duress is the desire to gain a quick end to an unpleasant situation. They would certainly not approach the same person again.

If you want to become a good seller who customers will be returning to, or if you're looking for suitable candidates who could become your salespeople, you should know that such a person:

- Is a good listener and tries to understand what the customer is interested in.
- Instead of talking too much tries to tune in to the client's needs and help him or her.
- Focuses on solving the customer's problem rather than on the profit from sales.
- Doesn't exert any pressure on the client ("You have to buy that skirt; it looks great on you!").
- Can ask the right questions, which in turn means that he or she will find out more about the customer and their needs.
- Welcomes every customer regardless of a potential sale.

"Negotiating with business partners didn't stress me at all, but I felt uncomfortable when I found I had to lead a team of employees – all of them men. I had experience with managerial work from my previous job, but I had only managed a group of women. I thought about how I could approach men so that they would take me seriously. After all, I am a woman leading a furniture company, which is rather unusual.

I even considered dying my blonde hair dark! After an embarrassing start, when I sensed amused expectations behind the facade of politeness, I pulled myself together and started talking fair and straight. I stopped worrying about what I would sound like if I said this or that and it worked. I don't go to the bar with my employees after work, but I think we have very good relationships."
(Nicole, 39, USA)

3. COMMUNICATE WITH YOUR EMPLOYEES

You need to have a team of people around you who will pull together. If you don't make all your employees pull in one direction, your boat will start wobbling and it won't be long before it capsizes. That's why you should tell your employees regularly about what is happening in your company, about your new ideas, business intentions and the promotional methods you've selected. Choose the form of communication that suits you best, whether that involves holding regular personal meetings or sending information by email. Let every employee know they are an indispensable part of your team and that you appreciate the work they're doing. Appreciate the effort beyond the scope of their duties in particular.

When informing your employees, be open, because this will encourage them to be open too. Then you'll have your ears to the ground in your company and, more than that, you'll get valuable feedback. Don't leave negative information out (bad economic results, a series of defective products, etc.), because it is better if they learn it from you than via the rumour mill in a distorted form. Phrase bleak communications constructively. Don't speak about inability or bad luck, but rather about reserves and future opportunities.

Keep the door to your office open (symbolically as well as literally) and don't overdo it with hierarchy and formal relationships. Constant monitoring of your employees is unnecessary if they are motivated enough to strive for your company's prosperity. Naturally, it is also about choosing the right people to entrust with competences and responsibility, and they will motivate themselves. In companies with long histories, the best employees often become managers or company partners.

4. BECOME A REAL LEADER

Work on becoming a respected leader. Leadership is a quality you need to develop from within yourself. That means the following:

SUBDUE YOUR FEAR
You need to be ready to go beyond your comfort zone, as safe and low goals are only set by people who don't believe in themselves.

BE CONFIDENT
Find the right position between proud and humble behaviour. Be confident and self-assured.

MAKE DECISIONS
You cannot afford to be indecisive. Not because of your image, but because decision making is and will be a daily occurrence from now on.

Don't hesitate too long before you return a verdict, and come to terms with the fact that sometimes you won't have as much information as you'd like. After you make a decision, don't waste your time or energy thinking about whether you did everything right or not and what others may think about it. You made the best decision you were able to make at the given moment.

STAND FIRM

Everyone around you will have an opinion or the best advice on what you should do or should have done. Be careful that the inflow of unsolicited advice doesn't distract you too much and you don't lose sight of what you want.

DARE TO FAIL

The way to success is not always straightforward and it isn't always smooth sailing. Obviously, not everything always ends well. Let yourself and your employees fail sometimes, and don't beat yourself up when it happens.

BE DISCIPLINED AND SEE THINGS THROUGH

Many natural entrepreneurs are endowed with a mind that is a perfect idea-making machine. The good news is that some of these ideas are money spinners. The bad news is that if you get carried away by every new idea, you'll never bring the old ones to a successful conclusion. Business discipline is not about effort, although that is important too. During my years working for Meriglobe Advisory House I met entrepreneurs who were far too creative. One of them even watched his successful company go bankrupt, as he focused each month on developing a new idea.

TAKE HEALTHY RISKS

If you want to hedge your bets, you won't get very far in business. You can, of course, offer the same chocolate cake in your cake shop every day if your customers adore it, but you need to change at least part of what you offer from time to time, knowing that each innovation brings new risks. However, it is also risky to delegate certain tasks to your colleagues, open a new shop or rely on a new technology. On the other hand, nobody forces you to fight every battle and take risks at all costs.

You can read about what a real leader should be like and what skills he or she should have, for instance, in numerous books such as Jo Owen's *How to Lead* (Pearson, 2011).

5. KEEP AN EYE ON YOUR COMPETITION

Even if you have a lot of work with your own company, don't forget to keep an eye on what your competition is doing. Otherwise, you won't ever know if you're doing enough to keep your current customers and win new ones. You can easily get information from the Internet, where you can find what your competition offers, how successful they are and what business practices they're using.

Evaluate the facts that you find and make relevant conclusions for yourself. However, don't let yourself be drawn too far into what somebody else is doing. This will use up your energy and take the wind out of your sails. Find inspiration, but don't get deviated from your course. Your offer is unique and that's why your customers keep returning to you. Imitating or copying somebody else will never make you happy, certainly not for long.

And there's something more. In this book I have urged you to use the Internet, including social media, as much as you can, and the truth is that modern technology can make your business significantly easier and more efficient. Now is the right time to add that this technology is not a magic bullet and it doesn't guarantee your success, even if the people around you try to make you believe something else. You actually have the most important things you need for a successful business with you all the time: an alert brain and an open heart.

"Now I'm happy that I didn't stay in the pharmacy as an employee, but opened my own. However, if I had known then how much work and effort it would cost me, I don't know if I would have found the courage to do it. The truth is, I underestimated the competition at the start – I opened my first pharmacy when the market was already saturated, and it took quite some time before I got regular customers. I was walking a tightrope, the money was draining away and the number of customers rose very slowly. I think I studied every marketing manual I got hold of at that time. But I also gained the most valuable experience."
(Camille, 45, Belgium)

6. DON'T EXPECT TO SUCCEED IMMEDIATELY

Forget about the films where the main hero implements his ingenious idea overnight and the next day he's a millionaire chased after by a crowd of eager clients. Even Mark Zuckerberg didn't find success so quickly with Facebook, and you probably won't be any faster. Building a company requires making a great effort, a lot of hard work and time. It may be months, probably even years, before you can tell yourself you've built the basis of a stable company.

Not everything you plant turns into a blossoming rose and not everything will go swimmingly. You'll face unpleasant situations, and there will be times when you'll feel stressed, overwhelmed by anxiety or fear. Don't be afraid to ask for help if you find yourself in such a situation. It is not a sign of your weakness, but rather of your internal strength. Trouble and partial failures are an inseparable part of a being an entrepreneur and you need to learn to take hard hits and turn them into challenges. Do you know the story about the oak and the willow?

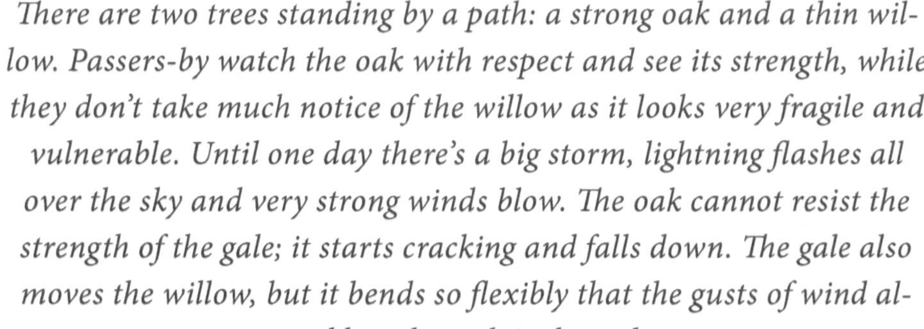

There are two trees standing by a path: a strong oak and a thin willow. Passers-by watch the oak with respect and see its strength, while they don't take much notice of the willow as it looks very fragile and vulnerable. Until one day there's a big storm, lightning flashes all over the sky and very strong winds blow. The oak cannot resist the strength of the gale; it starts cracking and falls down. The gale also moves the willow, but it bends so flexibly that the gusts of wind always blow through its branches.

In the world of business, you need to have the roots of an oak and the flexibility of a willow. Only then can you deal with what's to come.

7. ASSESS REGULARLY

No matter how bogged down you are with solving everyday problems in your company, or if you feel everything is running smoothly, you should take time to analyse and evaluate the results you have achieved over a certain period.

Set a regular frequency, say, once a month or four times a year, when you'll look at the accounting statements to see whether there is anything that needs to be corrected, changed or improved. This is the only way you can learn about adverse phenomena that manifest so slowly and creepingly that you wouldn't have the opportunity to notice them in time otherwise. You'll save yourself future trouble. And even if there's nothing undesirable going on, you can at least feast your eyes on the results of your work.

8. DON'T REST ON YOUR LAURELS

I wish from the bottom of my heart that you enjoy the fruits of your labour and appreciate yourself for what you've done. But don't stand rooted to one spot so that you can't move. The company needs your constant care in order to grow and develop.

Don't forget it is necessary to:

- Improve the quality of your customer service.
- Find new ways of promoting your company and its services or products.
- Develop new products to keep up with the times.
- Search for the information necessary to improve your business.
- Update your business plan.

9. FOSTER GOOD RELATIONSHIPS

You come into contact with people of various professions and you never know who may become your customer, employee, colleague or supplier. That doesn't mean you should reduce your interpersonal relationships to this single aspect. Take your business as an opportunity for your personal development, and take meeting the people you come across in business as inspiration and an opportunity to learn something about yourself and the world around you.

- Be honest and open, as that is the only way you can build a good name and reputation, which is priceless in life and business.
- Let people get to know you more. Don't be an enigmatic, anonymous or even invisible being for your customers. Be close to them in case they need you. Be friendly, smile and talk to them.
- Get involved in business associations and if there aren't any in your region, consider establishing a society where entrepreneurs of small and medium-sized businesses could meet you. Again, it will be an opportunity to network and exchange experiences and contacts.
- "Networking" is actually nothing other than establishing and building contacts that are crucial for a new company. In fact, you can extend the network of the people you know anywhere and anytime. All you need to do is to be alert, ask and be interested in others, they will certainly reward you with interesting information or recommendations.

Having a good network of contacts means not only winning new clients, but also finding suppliers or employees. It is vital that you are ready to respond to any new challenge or request. Collect contacts at

your own or somebody else's parties, social events, co-working centres, from social media, interest groups or professional associations.
(29)

You may be frightened by the idea of speaking in public or in front of a crowd. However, at the same time it is a chance to acquire new contacts that your business may benefit from and that is worth the few minutes of discomfort, isn't it?

10. THINK POSITIVELY

Our society highly appreciates critique and so-called common sense wisdom that is often mistaken for scepticism. Thinking positively doesn't equate to succumbing to inappropriate enthusiasm, being naive or wearing rose-tinted glasses and overlooking unpleasant facts, events or warnings. Thinking positively means seeing the glass as half full and treating obstacles, mistakes and failures as opportunities to start doing things differently.

Negative thoughts are not just a harmless mental game, but they are reflected in our reality. If you only expect negative things, you will find them. Now I'm not talking about everyday worries, as they are inseparable from business since business always carries a certain amount of risk. What I mean is the belief that it will all end badly. When you think positively, you attract positive results. That's why it is important to do what is often accentuated these days: accept responsibility for everything that is happening to you in your life.

Keep a positive mindset, even when your business is not doing very well, and try to build your faith in yourself and your business intentions. Company owners who are successful long term don't close their eyes to unpleasant facts, but they don't lose their faith in success either. If you want to read more about how to do it, there are many books available on this topic. For example:

- Gibson, A., *A Mind for Business: Get Inside Your Head to Transform How You Work* (Pearson, 2015).
- Mayher, B., *Filling the Glass: The Skeptic's Guide to Positive Thinking in Business* (Barry Maher & Associates, 2007).
- Newton, R., *The Little Book of Thinking Big* (Capstone Publishing, 2014).

11. ENTREPRENEUR IS JUST ONE OF YOUR ROLES IN LIFE

Even if your business is currently taking up 100 per cent of your time, don't forget it is only work, and work isn't everything. You also need to have some time just for yourself. I know, it is easier said than done when you feel like you don't have time to breathe. There are certainly times when you wake up and go to bed with business matters on your mind, and you have no capacity left for anything else. But it is important to slow down a little as soon as you can and have a rest (lazing around with a book, exercising, listening to music, etc.). A permanently high working tempo doesn't lead to achieving goals, but to burning out, and in the worst cases to developing an addiction (to alcohol, medications, etc.) or illness.

If you are to be successful in business over the long term, you must enjoy the work you're doing and it must fulfil you. However, you mustn't cling to it and see it as your only meaning in life. It is important to keep a good work–life balance and remember that you're not just a businesswoman, but also a mother, wife, daughter, sister, friend and so on. Reserve enough time for your children, family and friends. Take care of relationships with your relatives and friends as they are the ones who make up the safety net that will catch you and support you in times when your business is not doing so well. In better times these relationships will feed you with the energy you need to accomplish your dreams, private as well as professional ones.

QUESTIONS TO CONSIDER

**IN WHICH OF THE ABOVE STATED AREAS
DO I HAVE WEAKNESSES?**
Choose only two or three areas to focus on and try to improve, otherwise you risk splintering your concentration and strengths.

HOW IMPORTANT IS BUSINESS IN MY LIFE?
Is it important enough for you? Does it make you forget other life values?

AFTERWORD

They say that chance favours the prepared mind. And you are prepared. You know everything you need to know about business at this moment, and I believe that you have the confidence and determination to make your dream come true.

I would be pleased if you sent your observations, ideas and stories to me at **alexandra@alexandrajohn.com**.

I wish you a safe journey!

ALEXANDRA JOHN
Prague, London (December 2017)

Appendix

What you might find useful

Where to go for further information and inspiration

The aim of this book has been to provide you with the information you need when considering and setting your business intentions, establishing your company and starting up your business. I believe it includes useful references to other sources from which you can draw everything you need so that you are ready to face whatever you may come across in the beautiful and mysterious jungle of business.

Most importantly, I would like to invite you to visit my website **www.alexandrajohn.com** where you can find a lot of articles on various aspects of business.

REFERENCES

1. Ovládnou ženy byznys 21. století? (Are Women Dominating 21st-Century Business?)
   www.amsp.cz/ovladnou-zeny-byznys-21-stoleti

2. www.femaleentrepreneurassociation.com/2014/05/building-a-virtual-assistant-business/

3. Why You Should Start a Business Now
   www.maxfilings.com/incorporation-knowledge-center/why-start-a-business-now.php

4. Ženy, kterým miliardy nespadly do klína (The Women whose Billions didn't Just Fall into their Laps)
   www.novinky.cz/zena/styl/205313-zeny-kterym-miliardy-nespadly-do-klina.html

5. www.psidetektiv.cz

6. Don't be Afraid to Take a Risk
   www.femaleentrepreneurassociation.com/2014/08/dont-be-afraid-to-take-a-risk/

7. 5 Steps to Building a Successful Niche Business
   www.entrepreneur.com/article/202900

8. An Introduction to Business Plans
   www.entrepreneur.com/article/38290

9. What's an Angel Investor?
   www.wsj.com/articles/SB10001424052702303491304575188420191459904

10. www.gov.uk/government/news/new-enterprise-allowance-unleashes-a-wave-of-entrepreneurs

11. Jumping from Finance to Fashion
    www.femaleentrepreneurassociation.com/2014/09/jumping-from-finance-to-fashion/

12. Making the Decision to Hire: Balancing Financial Considerations and Business Needs
    www.bizfilings.com/toolkit/sbg/office-hr/hiring-workers/making-the-decision-to-hire.aspx

13. 10 chyb při pohovorech s uchazeči (1. díl) (10 Mistakes to Avoid When Interviewing Job Applicants (Part 1))
    www.podnikatel.cz/clanky/10-chyb-pri-pohovorech-s-uchazeci-1-dil/

14. Martha Stewart 3.0, aneb jak rozjet úspěšný byznys (Martha Stewart 3.0, or How to Start a Successful Business)
    www.lupa.cz/clanky/martha-stewart-3-0-aneb-jak-rozjet-uspesny-byznys/

15. Psychologie barev: jaké poselství nese vaše logo (Psychology of Colour: What Message Does your Logo Carry)
www.personalni-marketing.cz/detail-clanku/psychologie-barev-jake-poselstvi-nesevase-logo-cast1

16. www.femaleentrepreneurassociation.com/2014/06/just-start-your-own-business-now/

17. Nielsen: global consumers' trust in 'earned' advertising grows in importance
www.nielsen.com/us/en/press-room/2012/nielsen-global-consumers-trust-in-earned-advertising-grows.html

18. Godfrey and Gregory Harris, 101 způsobů, jak propagovat svou fi rmu (101 Ways to Promote Your Business), Príroda 1999

19. www.statista.com/statistics/272014/global-social-networks-ranked-by-number-of-users/

20. www.brandwatch.com/2016/05/37-instagram-stats-2016/

21. www.globalwebindex.net/blog/4-in-10-internet-users-are-linkedin-members

22. www.techtimes.com/articles/51205/20150506/many-users-google-really.htm#sthash.pV8Bq4mA.dpuf

23. www.socialmediatoday.com/content/blogging-more-important-today-ever

24. How to Make Your Business Last 100 Years
www.entrepreneur.com/blog/218975

25. Smutek Coco Chanel sluší (Sadness Suits Coco Chanel)
www.krasnapani.cz/casopis-krasna/clanky-online/osobnosti-a-rozhovory/396

26. Target Resources to Get Marketing Right
www.theguardian.com/small-business-network/2013/jun/05/marketing-small-business-budget

27. Kosmetické dynastie (Cosmetic Dynasty)
www.elle.cz/krasa/pece-o-telo-a-plet/kosmeticke-dynastie

28. The 7 C's: How to Find and Hire Great Employees
www.forbes.com/sites/alanhall/2012/06/19/the-7-cs-how-to-find-and-hire-great-employees/#4e644bef2b29

29. Pracovní networking: rozhoďte sítě s kontakty (Working Networking: Spread the Word with Contacts)
www.vkancelari.cz/2013/pracovni-networking-rozhodte-site-kontakty

Notes:

BE YOUR OWN BOSS OR BECOME A BUSINESSWOMAN IN 30 DAYS

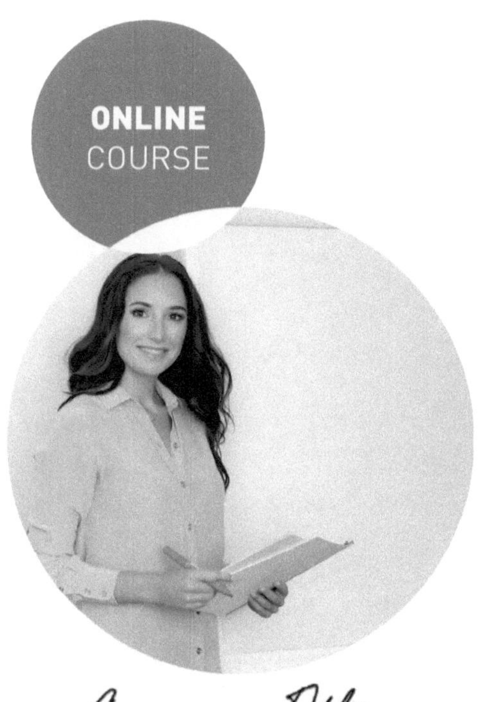

Follow up the book with an online course where you will learn:

1. Can I become a businesswoman?

2. How do I come up with a good business idea?

3. How do I develop a product from my idea?

4. How do I find customers and make a product that will meet their needs?

5. How and why should I write a business plan?

6. How do I finance my business?

7. How do I find a product or service provider? How do I know which are reliable?

8. What is networking and how can I make use of it?

9. How do I communicate with customers online and sell successfully?

10. How do I communicate with customers offline and sell successfully? How can I be successful when communicating face2face?

Go to: alexandrajohn.com/course

ALEXANDRA JOHN
Being your own boss
How to start up a business

Graphic design, typesetting: David Obdržálek, Hana Melčová, Jan Jindra
Proofreading: Francesca White, Rebecca Hollinger

First edition, 2017
ISBN: 978-80-906584-0-0